I0555407

THE CONFIDENT

Postpartum

YOUR GUIDE TO THRIVING IN MOTHERHOOD

KRYSTA SCHROEDER, LCSW–QS, PMH–C AND SARAH MULLINAX, LCSW

FULFILLING MOTHERHOOD BY HARLOWE COUNSELING

To Ezra, Wren, and Charlie,

The little sparks that ignited a fire within us, to embrace our dreams of motherhood, and become the mothers we have always aspired to be.

We love you.

Fulfilled Mama

A mother who stands tall in her confidence and empowerment. She is a woman who understands that there's no one-size-fits-all approach to motherhood, and thus, she embraces it in her own unique way. She is an individual, not defined by societal expectations or generic norms. Rather, she sets her own standards and paves her own path, radiating assurance and contentment. She is a beacon of self-assuredness, a testament to the power of individuality, and the embodiment of motherly love. She is a symbol of strength, resilience, and unconditional love.

HELLO, DEAR FRIENDS!

Welcome to "The Confident Postpartum", a journey we are both honored and thrilled to share with you. Your choice to let us accompany you on this transformative path is one we deeply appreciate.

In the pages of this workbook, you'll discover the wisdom, insights, and advice we wish we'd had as we stepped into our roles as mothers. It's filled with the highs and lows, the triumphs and trials, the joy and the jitters that come with embracing motherhood.

While we can't promise a magic formula that will make motherhood a breeze, what we can assure you is this – by the end of this workbook, you'll feel empowered, ready, and above all, confident to face the multifaceted journey that is motherhood.

This workbook is more than just a guide; it's a companion, designed to support you through every stage of your postpartum journey. We've poured our hearts, personal experiences, and professional expertise into these pages, hoping to make your transition into motherhood smoother and more joyful. With support and preparation, we hope to empower you with the confidence and knowledge you need to step into this new role and be the Fulfilled Mama you want to be!

We eagerly await hearing about your experiences, triumphs, and how you've grown in confidence throughout this journey. Remember, there's no 'perfect' way to be a mother, but countless ways to be a great one. Here's to your journey into confident motherhood. We're with you every step of the way.

Warmly,

Krysta & Sarah

contents

contents

CHAPTER ONE

BRINGING YOUR AUTHENTIC SELF TO MOTHERHOOD:

Exploring Your Likes, Dislikes, Beliefs, and Values

We're ready to embark on this journey with you. Whether you're contemplating motherhood, in the throes of pregnancy, newly postpartum, or a seasoned mother, this book is designed with you in mind. It aims to facilitate self-reflection and assist you in sculpting your ideal motherhood experience. Don't hesitate to bypass any topics or queries that don't resonate at the moment. You can always circle back when you feel prepared. Your individuality is what sets you apart as a mother. Without further ado, let's dive in.

Getting to know yourself!

As mothers, we bring our whole selves to the role, both in who we've been and who we are becoming. Things change, but at our core, we remain ourselves. For many of us, once the initial postpartum haze dissipates, we find ourselves feeling disoriented, questioning who we are now, and trying to figure out who this new version of ourselves is. No two moms are the same and we believe the key to confidence in motherhood is embracing your uniqueness. This chapter aims to serve as an anchor for you, a guide in exploring your authentic self in motherhood.

By taking the time to reflect on these prompts, you're not only gaining a clearer understanding of who you are, but also building a foundation to navigate the changes and challenges of motherhood. These are the building blocks we will build on in the chapters ahead.

In this upcoming section, we will explore:
- Who you are now
- Your needs
- Connecting with others
- Your likes and dislikes
- Creating a space that makes you feel most like yourself

Grab a pen or pencil, let's get started!

Section One: Embracing the Now

Let's start with understanding who you are at this moment. We'll use journal prompts to dive deep into your thoughts and feelings, providing a snapshot of your current life.

1 What three ordinary things bring you the most joy?

2 What are your favorite hobbies? Why?

3 What are a few of your favorite thing about yourself?

Section Two: Understanding Your Needs

In this section, we'll explore how you recharge, how you handle difficult situations, and what aspects of life make you feel vulnerable or uncertain.

1 How do you encourage yourself when trying something new?

2 What helps you slow down and be more present?

3 How do you notice you're nearing burnout?

Section Three: Connecting With Others

Here, we'll delve into your relationships, examining how you share your feelings, your preferred ways of socializing, and who gets to see the most authentic version of you.

1 How do you share your feelings with people who care about you?

2 How do you like to spend time with your friends/family?

3 Who sees the most authentic version of you?

Section Four: Exploring Likes and Dislikes

This section enables you to reflect on your likes and dislikes, from everyday activities and self care methods to traits in people and preferred personal spaces.

1   What are your favorite parts of your day?

2   How do you like the space around you like your home or daily surroundings?

3   What are your biggest pet peeves and trigger points? This can be in people, noises, etc.

Section Five: Recognizing Your "You" Space

Finally, we'll identify your 'you space'—the circumstances under which you feel most like yourself—and explore what you need during times of stress or illness.

1 Where, when, and with whom do you feel most like yourself?

2 What do you normally need when you don't feel well or are under major stress?

Moving into this next chapter, we will be exploring the concept of self care in motherhood. We often hear about self care referencing things like massages or getting our nails done. Although those can be self care, at the heart of self care is an understanding of who YOU are and what YOU need to feel whole, happy, and cared for. We encourage you to reflect on any themes that came up in your journal entry responses above as you move forward in this book.

Bringing Your Authentic Self to Motherhood

"BE SO AUTHENTIC THAT OTHERS ARE NOT AFRAID TO BE THEMSELVES, TOO."

CHAPTER TWO

EMPOWERING YOUR INNER SELF:

Cultivating Personal Identity, the Art of Self-Care,

and Discovering Your Personal Boundaries

As we introduced at the end of our last chapter, self care is taking the time to engage in activities that better your physical and mental health. We often see self care as activities like going to the gym, going for a massage, or getting a hair cut. All of those things can be self care but there is so much more to self care.

The interesting thing about self care is, like beauty, self care is in the eye of the beholder. It is all about what helps YOU feel better physically and emotionally. Did you know there are different kinds of self care? Let's break it down!

Self-Care Activities Examples

EMOTIONAL

- journaling
- listening to music
- therapy
- talking about your feelings

MENTAL/COGNITIVE

- puzzles
- reading
- learning something new
- watching a documentary

PHYSICAL

- eating well
- getting good sleep
- healthy movement (as you can)
- medical follow up

SOCIAL

- connecting with family or friends
- setting boundaries
- balance alone time
- be aware of comparison (social media, immediate social circle)

PRACTICAL

- maintaining your home (however you can)
- budget planning
- making plans that work for you
- asking for help

SPIRITUAL

Connecting with something bigger than you through:
- connecting with nature
- community groups
- volunteering
- praying
- meditation

Section Two: Setting Ourselves Up for Success with Realistic Expectations

So we've identified the types of self care and some examples of activities that help promote self care, but we can't do all of those things every day or even every week, right? Of course not.

Let's imagine our daily capacity to engage in self care much like that of a traffic light; green, yellow, and red. Let's explore what each of these represents in regards to self care.

Green Light - Ideal Self Care

This represents days when everything aligns perfectly - you have time, energy, your kids are cooperative, you had a good night's sleep, and you have plenty of support available. On these days, you can fully charge your 'self care battery' by indulging in activities that nourish your body, mind, and soul. This could be things like a full workout session, a long relaxing bath, reading a book, or meditating.

Yellow Light - Moderate Self Care

These are the days when you face some challenges, maybe you're a bit tired, your kids require more attention, or you don't have as much support. You can still recharge your 'self care battery', but maybe not to 100%. Activities could include a short walk, a quick yoga session, a few minutes of deep breathing, or even just a hot cup of tea in peace.

Red Light - Quick and Easy Self Care

This represents the days when circumstances are tough - you're exhausted, time is scarce, kid conflicts are high, and support is low. Charging your 'self care battery' might seem impossible, but even on these days, it's important to find small ways to care for yourself. This could be as simple as taking a few deep breaths, listening to a favorite song, taking a shower, or even just savoring a few moments of quiet once the kids are in bed.

Empowering Your Inner Self

Section Three: Who Are You Outside of Relationships and Roles?

In this section, we will continue this journey of self-discovery and explore the question, "Who are you?" Beyond the roles of being a mother, a daughter, a significant other, a friend, there is a unique individual with dreams, passions, and qualities that make you who you are. We will delve into understanding your true essence and uncovering the aspects of your identity that go beyond societal expectations and labels. Let's explore!

1 Have you ever wondered how others perceive you? If you were to ask your partner, best friend, or parents to describe you, what would they say?

2 Exploring your passions outside of your roles as a mother and partner allows you to connect with your authentic self. What are you most proud of about yourself?

3 Finally, what are the activities that ignite a fire within you? Are there activities, spaces, or challenges that excite you and make you feel like the best version of you?

So, why does all this matter? As we embark on the journey of motherhood, we often find ourselves engrossed in creating endless lists of things to buy or skills to acquire. However, amidst all the planning and preparation, we sometimes overlook our most valuable asset – ourselves.

Remember, you already possess the most crucial element needed for this journey – your unique self. By keeping your own wellbeing and personal growth at the forefront of your mind, we can tap into your innate strengths, confront any beliefs or habits that may hinder you from living your best life, and help you reconnect with your individuality whenever you feel adrift.

Motherhood doesn't require perfection; it requires you – in your most authentic, empowered form. So let's start by nurturing the woman who makes all the magic happen. After all, a thriving mother is at the heart of a thriving family.

Empowering Your Inner Self

SELF CARE STOP LIGHT

Now that you have an idea of the things that you enjoy, let's take a minute to break out what an Ideal, Moderate, and Quick and Easy Self Care day will look like for you. Having this will help take the mental load out of planning out your self care. Simply Identify what color day it is and follow the plan you have already set.

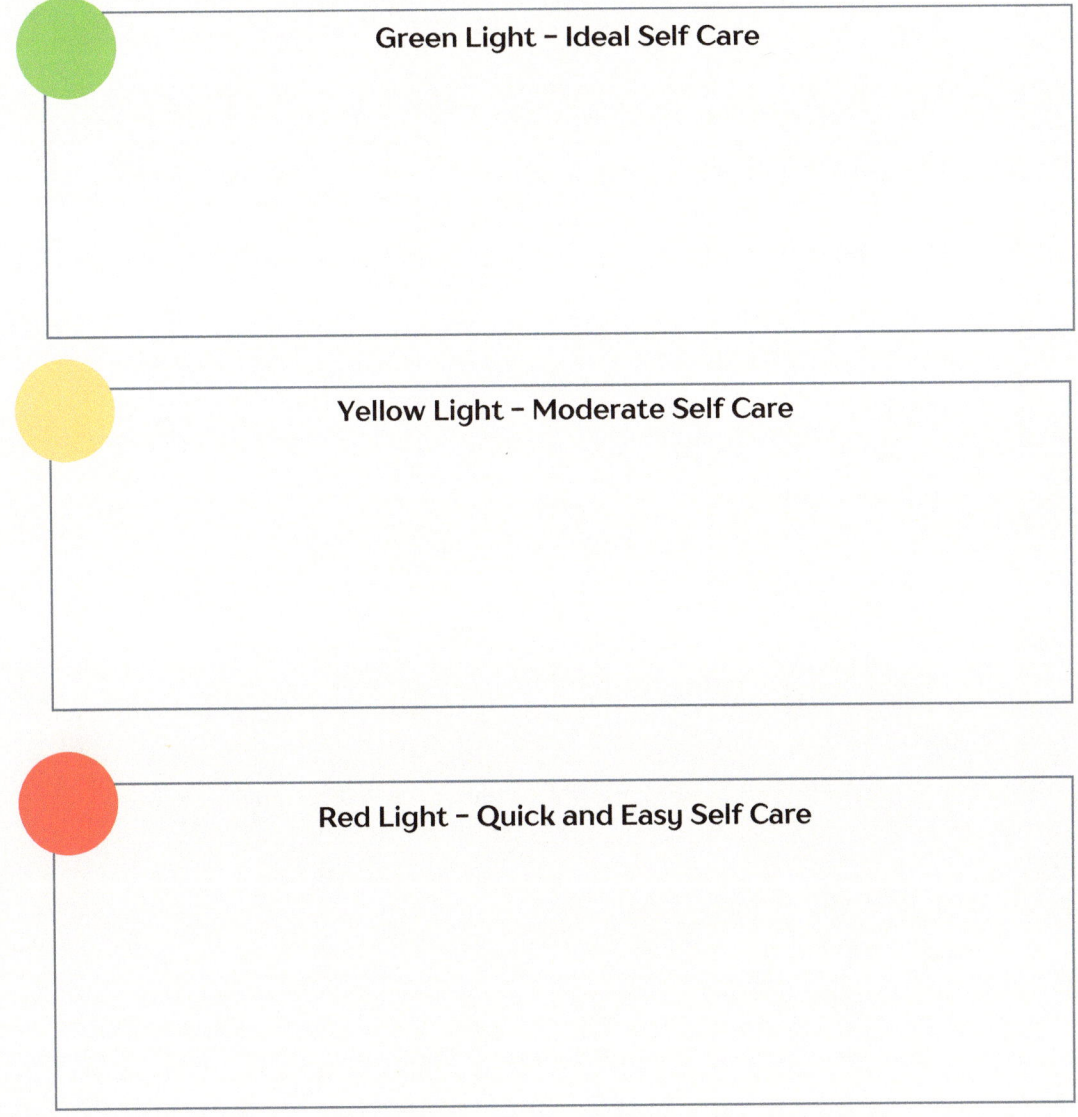

Green Light – Ideal Self Care

Yellow Light – Moderate Self Care

Red Light – Quick and Easy Self Care

Section Four: How We Talk to Ourselves

There's one more very important piece of self care and that is how we talk to ourselves! Most of us talk negatively to ourselves at least sometimes. This negative self talk can almost feel automatic. One really good way to start shifting the way we talk to ourselves is with positive affirmations. We have listed a few below. We encourage you to write down any that speak to you and post them somewhere you can see. That could be on a board or sign during birth, on sticky notes, in an alarm on your phone, or on your refrigerator. Maybe all of them!

- I am doing my best as a mom and that is enough.

- I am the best mom for my children; I was born to be their mom.

- Mistakes and setbacks are stepping stones in my journey because I learn from them.

- Only I can give my children a happy mother.

- I am my child's lifelong teacher.

- I will talk about myself the way I would my best friend.

- I will take care of myself in order to be a good mother.

- Being a mother has shown me how strong I am.

Empowering Your Inner Self

"SELF-CARE IS NOT SELFISH."

CHAPTER THREE

ANCHORING PARENTHOOD:

The Art of Establishing Family Values and

Crafting Healthy Boundaries

As you embark on the journey of parenthood, have you pondered over the idea of establishing a core set of family values? These values act as a compass, guiding your family's actions and interactions. It's easy to perceive family values as abstract concepts, yet they become concrete when we tie our parenting choices back to these foundational principles. In fact, aligning our decisions with established values is one of the most impactful strategies for confident family decision-making, from infancy through to adulthood.

In this chapter, we will demystify the concept of family values, helping you identify and articulate your own. We'll provide insights on how to make family decisions that are grounded in these core values. Remember, the values you establish today may evolve over time; that's perfectly normal and healthy. However, entering parenthood with a clear path will make it significantly easier to remain true to the vision you have for your family.

Understanding Family Values

Understanding family values is like uncovering the heart of your family, the core beliefs that guide your daily actions and decisions. These values are the principles that you want to instill in your children, shaping their character and influencing their behavior. They're the unwritten rules that define what your family stands for, often shaping the way you interact with each other and the world.

As you navigate the journey of parenthood, articulating your family values and forging an agreement with your spouse or co-parent becomes a powerful tool. This shared understanding lays a strong foundation for decision-making within your family.

When confronted with a choice, you can pause and ask yourself: "Is the pressure I'm feeling rooted in our established family values, or is it external pressure from other sources?"

This level of introspection empowers you to discern between your genuine values and external influences, enabling you to make decisions confidently and in alignment with what truly matters to your family. It's like having a compass that always points you back to your family's core principles, no matter the situation at hand.

Now, let's delve deeper into how to establish these values as a family. Remember, this process is not about creating rigid rules but about nurturing a shared understanding that grows and evolves with your family. It's about identifying the principles that reflect who you are as a family and who you aspire to be.

Establishing Family Values

As we embark on the journey of identifying and listing your family values, we thought it would be beneficial to share a list of 25 potential family values as a starting point. Remember, the number of values that resonate with you will be unique to your family. However, we suggest focusing on no more than 5 top-priority values during this process.

Our aim is to help you zero in on what truly matters to you and your family. We want to assist you in capturing the essence of what you hold dear, what you value most as a family unit. This exercise isn't about adhering to a prescribed set of values; rather, it's about discovering and embracing the principles that genuinely reflect your family's identity and aspirations.

25 Examples of Family Values

1. **Respect:** Treating each other with kindness and consideration.
2. **Honesty:** Valuing truthfulness and integrity.
3. **Responsibility:** Encouraging accountability for actions.
4. **Empathy:** Understanding and sharing the feelings of others.
5. **Compassion:** Offering kindness and understanding to others.
6. **Patience:** Accepting delay or difficulty without getting angry.
7. **Generosity:** Being willing to give and share unselfishly.
8. **Loyalty:** Showing constant support to each other.
9. **Gratitude:** Expressing appreciation for each other's efforts.
10. **Cooperation:** Working together towards common goals.
11. **Adaptability:** Being flexible in the face of change.
12. **Courage:** Standing up for what is right, even when it's hard.
13. **Perseverance:** Persisting in a course of action despite obstacles.
14. **Forgiveness:** Letting go of grudges and resentment.
15. **Self-discipline:** Practicing control over one's own actions.
16. **Creativity:** Encouraging imagination and original ideas.
17. **Humility:** Maintaining a modest view of one's own importance.
18. **Optimism:** Upholding a positive outlook on life.
19. **Curiosity:** Encouraging a desire to learn and explore.
20. **Healthy Communication:** Promoting open and honest conversation.
21. **Quality Time:** Prioritizing shared experiences and activities.
22. **Tradition:** Honoring family rituals and celebrations.
23. **Education:** Placing importance on learning and intellectual growth.
24. **Cleanliness:** Teaching respect and care for your environment.
25. **Work-Life Balance:** Balancing personal life and professional commitments

Now it's your turn! We recommend completing this section with your partner. Remember, it's okay if your values don't align perfectly; the key is to find common ground.

1

Reflect on your personal values
What principles have guided you throughout your life?
Which qualities do you admire in others?

2

What qualities do you most admire in your self and each other?

3

How do we want to treat each other within our family?
How do we want to engage with the world?

4   What are the non-negotiable behaviors in our home?

5   What qualities do we want our children to develop as they grow up?

6   **Let's Prioritize The Values You Have Written Down**
Which values are non-negotiable? Which ones are nice-to-have?

THE _____

FAMILY VALUES

ESTABLISHED ON:

1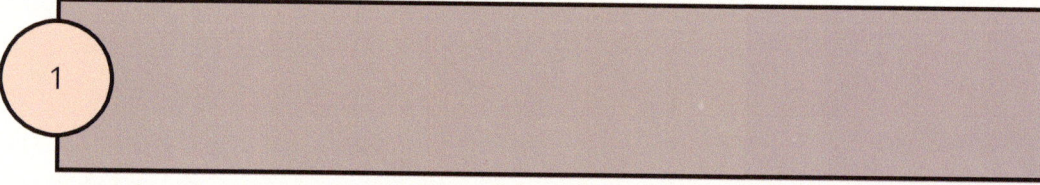

2

3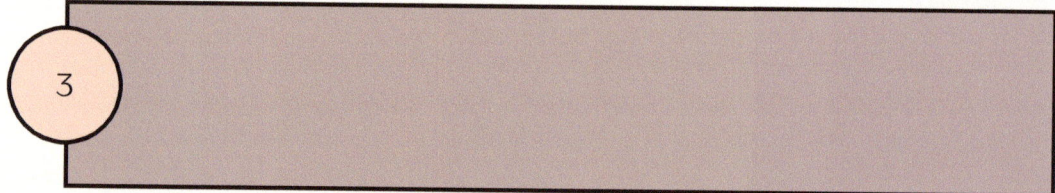

4

5

Anchoring Parenthood

Crafting Your Personal Boundaries

In our previous discussions, we've acknowledged the variety of beliefs and values that color our lives, impact our choices, and guide our decision-making. Our personal values also impact our relationships. In the same way values help guide our decisions, boundaries help protect those values and non-negotiables we have identified for ourselves and allow us to relate to those around us in a way that feels safe and respectful. As we embark on a deeper understanding of boundary setting and communication during the postpartum period, it's crucial to first explore the various types of relationships we have. Each differs in terms of the level of disclosure we're comfortable with and the intimacy we share.

As we embark on this journey, let's delve into the fascinating dynamics of our relationships, each distinguished by varying degrees of emotional intimacy. We'll explore the choices we make about what to share and with whom, shedding light on the boundaries we set with different individuals in our lives. On the following page, take a few moments to think about the people in your life, the differences of how vulnerable we can be with them, and if we have different unspoken rules between them.

The People in My Life

1. Center Circle- this is your immediate bubble. These are the people you share everything with. This doesn't mean you don't have boundaries in these relationships, but you feel comfortable and emotionally intimate.

2. Second Circle- these individuals are still very close but you may not share everything with them. The boundaries and communication with them may look different than your immediate bubble.

3. Continue moving out as you explore relationships that are less emotionally intimate and may require firmer boundaries.

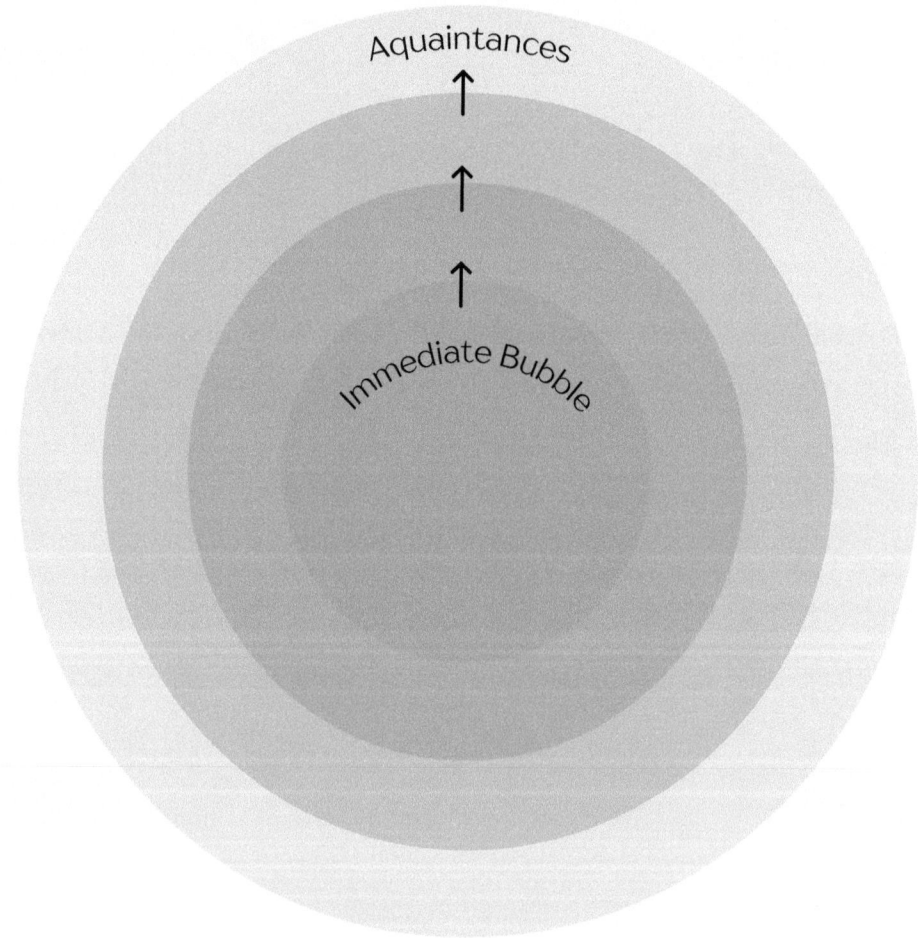

Boundary Setting

It's important to note that boundaries may be different with different "levels" of your relationships, as noted on the previous page. When thinking about a boundary, we often have the image of setting a harsh line or rule others have to abide by or else. In reality, we are simply communicating what we view as behavior we will receive or not receive, what makes us feel safe or unsafe, and what makes us feel able to be in relationship with those around us in a healthy way. Let's take a look at three concepts that often get confused for one another:

- **Rules**: Guidelines that aim to dictate behavior for individuals or groups.
- **Threats**: Using the possibility of punishment to control behavior.
- **Boundaries**: Communicating your personal response to a behavior, focusing on what you will or won't do. They protect your physical, emotional, and mental wellbeing.

NOTE: Boundaries are about you and your response to behavior. No one can dictate or control your boundaries. Although we desire for those around us to respect our boundaries, others response to our boundaries does not invalidate the boundaries that we have set.

The goal of establishing boundaries is not to control the behavior of those around us, cut people out, or set harsh rules. It is to create dynamics that feel healthy and fulfilling for us.

Let's take a look at an example:

Rule: No kissing the baby on the face.

Threat: If you kiss the baby on the face we won't come to your birthday dinner.

Boundary: If you kiss the baby on the face, I will not allow you to hold the baby.

Although the threat and boundary may feel similar, a boundary identifies what you will do to maintain comfort and safety in a situation. A threat is a punishment for the behavior.

Personal Space: Defining physical and emotional boundaries for yourself and others.

Time Management: Establishing limits on commitments, allowing time for self care and personal pursuits.

Emotional Well-being: Setting boundaries around toxic relationships or situations that drain your energy.

Communication: Clarifying how you want to be spoken to and treated in conversations.

Work-Life Balance: Ensuring a healthy separation between work and personal life.

Social Media: Regulating screen time and privacy settings to protect your mental wellbeing.

1   What are some boundaries that are important to you now in your day to day life?

2 Think about two different relationships in your life (your spouse vs your coworker maybe), and the differences of boundaries in both of relationships.

3 Dynamics change after having a baby, are there any boundaries you can foresee changing as you become a mother?

4 Are there any relationships in your life right now that you think would benefit from clearer boundaries?

"BOUNDARIES DON'T KEEP PEOPLE OUT, THEY SHOW THEM WHERE THE DOOR IS."

CHAPTER FOUR

SHATTERING LIMITING BELIEFS AND EMBRACING THE POWER OF SUPPORT

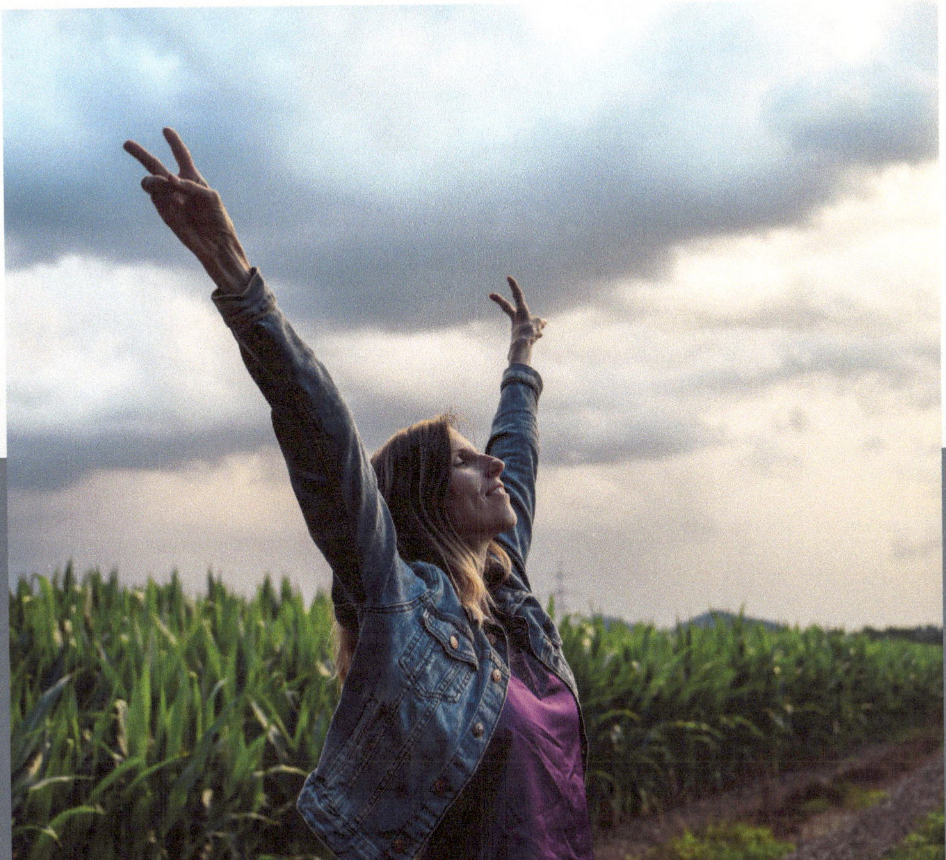

Beliefs That impact Us in Motherhood

We all come to motherhood with certain beliefs whether we realize it or not. Some seem obvious and natural and some may be so deeply held you don't even realize you believe it. Why does this matter? Our beliefs impact the way we see the world and the way we make sense of experiences.

This can impact the way we view ourselves as mothers, our expectations, and our ability to accept help. In this chapter, we will work through identifying these beliefs and determining how these beliefs shape how you will approach motherhood.

The journey of motherhood often brings with it the challenge of internal perfectionism, limiting beliefs, and external pressures for perfection. This chapter breaks down the concept and offers strategies to combat this often debilitating mindset.

Section One: The Fear of Relinquishing Control

One major factor contributing to resistance to asking for help is the fear of relinquishing control. As new mothers, we often worry about what might happen if we let go of certain tasks or responsibilities. These fears can range from concerns over the baby's wellbeing to anxiety about housework not being done precisely as we'd like.

But is there a way we can communicate these fears and make a plan to be able to receive support? Absolutely! Open communication about your worries with your partner, family, or support group can help alleviate some of these fears. Planning, delegating, and accepting that things may not always be perfect can pave the way for a more balanced, less stressful motherhood experience.

Section Two: Core Beliefs and Their Impact

Core beliefs are deeply held convictions that shape our perception of ourselves, others, and the world around us. They're often influenced by cultural/social norms or community/personal expectations of motherhood. Think of these beliefs like glasses through which we view any given situation. If the glasses are tinted with unrealistic expectations or harsh judgments, our perspective can become distorted. These beliefs can come from our own experiences, our culture, our families, or a combination of many sources. These beliefs can impact the way we view ourselves, our role as mothers, asking for help, parenting decisions, and so much more. This is where redefining our core beliefs becomes crucial

Let's take a look at an example:

Imagine your core beliefs as glasses through which you view your situation. If these glasses are tinted with the belief that parents should be able to handle all aspects of child care independently, and that asking for help would burden others, the picture can look bleak. You may feel like a failure if you can't do it all alone, and fear being seen as a bad mom because you can't meet these unrealistic expectations.

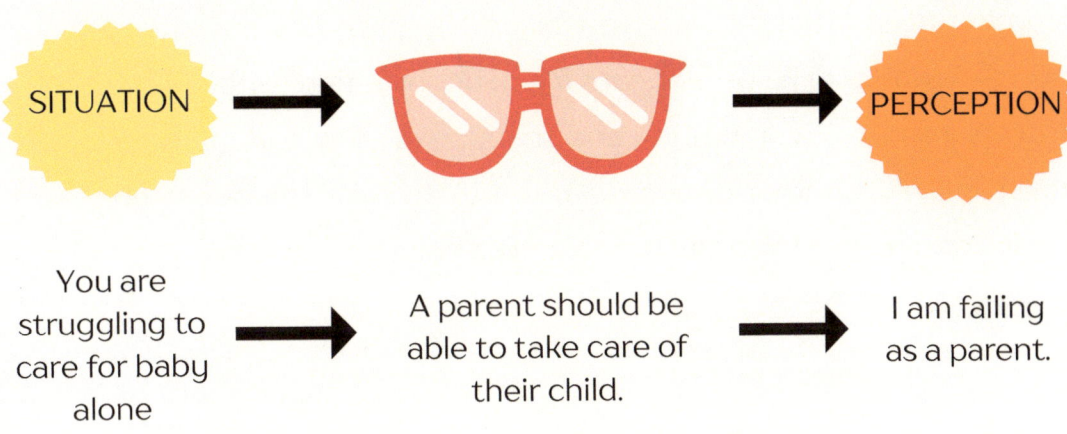

SITUATION → PERCEPTION

You are struggling to care for baby alone → A parent should be able to take care of their child. → I am failing as a parent.

But what if you could change your glasses? What if you could view your situation through lenses that reflect the wisdom of the adage, "It takes a village"? By shifting your core belief to understand that you are worthy of support, and that seeking help is actually a way of caring for your child, the whole scenario changes. You're no longer burdening others; rather, you're drawing from your resources and supports.

SITUATION

You are struggling to care for baby alone

It takes a village to raise a child and I am deserving of support.

PERCEPTION

I am drawing from my supports to best care for my baby and myself.

The consequences of this shift in perspective are profound. Instead of feeling inadequate, you open yourself up to receiving support and learning from others who have walked the path of parenthood before you. This not only helps you care for your child more effectively but also fosters a sense of community and shared experience. Remember, asking for help isn't a sign of weakness, but a testament to your strength and dedication to providing the best for your child.

Let's practice!

Let's work on rewriting some commonly held beliefs in motherhood that are often not true. You have likely heard these before and, while they can be true for some, they are not true for all. The goal here is to practice reframing thoughts and doubts by exploring the underlying belief, that way when you encounter a situation that you begin to have self-doubt in, you can reframe Into an empowering mindset.

Example Thoughts About the Situation:

I should know how to get my baby to stop crying and go to sleep.

Step 1: Identify Underlying Belief

Mother's Intuition helps you know how to do everything perfect from the start.

Step 2: Question the Belief:

Are there alternative beliefs? Where did this belief come from? Is this belief always 100% true? What if the opposite were true?

Step 3: List Alternative Belief(s)

Caring for a baby is like other skills that have to be learned. Some may come more naturally than others.

Reframed View of the Situation

I am learning about how my baby likes to be soothed, he is only 3 days old, it is okay that I am still learning. I am still a great mom.

Section Three: Externally Reinforced Beliefs
The Myth of the "Romanticized Version of Motherhood"

We all have a unique set of personal beliefs that are shaped by various influences - our experiences, cultural background, familial values, and much more. However, there are certain belief systems that echo louder in our society, shared and perpetuated by a significant portion of our culture. One such belief system revolves around the perception of motherhood.

In today's digital age, social media has become a powerful tool in shaping societal beliefs. It acts as a mirror reflecting the good, the bad, and the ugly of our world, but often, this mirror is selectively polished to highlight only the good. This selective showcasing is particularly evident in the portrayal of motherhood on these platforms.

Scroll through any social media feed, and you'll find picture-perfect images of mothers cradling their babies, their faces glowing with pure joy. Homes are immaculate, meals are nutritious and beautifully plated, and every moment seems to be filled with laughter, love, and harmony. This curated narrative crafts an image of motherhood that is unblemished by hardships or struggles. It shows women who appear to be perfectly fulfilling the role of "mother".

While there's no denying that motherhood is indeed beautiful, this social media portrayal is incomplete. It's like looking at a rainbow but only seeing one color. The reality of motherhood is a spectrum of emotions and experiences — it's not just sunshine and rainbows but also stormy clouds and thunderstorms. There are sleepless nights, overwhelming days, moments of self-doubt, and feelings of inadequacy.

Shattering Limiting Beliefs and Embracing the Power of Support

When we only see the 'sunshine and rainbows' part of motherhood, it's easy to judge ourselves harshly when our own experience doesn't match up. We may start to feel like failures. What we often forget is that what we see on social media is a highlight reel, not a comprehensive documentary.

It's important to note that social media isn't the root cause of this issue. Rather, it serves as a platform that reinforces these societal norms. It amplifies the chasm between the image of 'picture-perfect' motherhood and the reality experienced by many mothers who feel they don't measure up to this high standard.

As a society, we have come to accept a certain image of motherhood. The ideal mother is portrayed as self-sacrificing, always putting her child's needs before her own. She is seen as a superwoman, capable of juggling all her previous responsibilities while embracing motherhood with a constant smile. In addition to this, she is expected to handle everything single-handedly. In our individualistic society that focuses on nuclear families with mothers as the caregivers, moms feel like they have to do it all. This unrealistic expectation creates an immense pressure on mothers, leading to feelings of inadequacy and failure when they can't live up to this idealized image.

The danger lies not in the existence of these images, but in our comparison and judgment of ourselves and others based on them. It's crucial to remember that it's okay to have 'cloudy' days. It's okay to struggle. It's not only okay but necessary and beautiful to be a real, human mother – not a picture-perfect social media construct. It is our uniqueness and authenticity that allows us to be truly fulfilled.

Let's take a moment to reflect.

1 Imagine the "perfect mother". What are some words you would use to describe her?

2 Where does this image of a perfect mother come from and are these described attributes necessary to be a good mother?

3 What do you think makes someone a good mother?

Have you heard of the "good enough mother"?

In 1953, British pediatrician and psychoanalyst Donald Winnicott coined the term "good enough mother" to express the importance of mothers letting go of perfectionism and embracing the idea that being "good enough" is sufficient for their child's development. This concept highlights the significance of emotionally holding children and providing them with a safe space to develop attachment by being consistently responsive to their emotions.

In the sometimes stressful and uncertain transition into motherhood, it can be easy to lose sight of yourself, your beliefs, and what is important to you. When we're not feeling optimal, whether that's stress, lack of sleep, poor nutrition, or adapting to new challenges, it is easy to lose sight of our personal beliefs and values. In the next chapter, we will discuss one of the most important skills for postpartum and beyond: communication. This important skill will help you express your needs, nurture your relationships, and have the fulfilling motherhood experience you desire. Although preparation cannot guarantee there will be no stress or uncertainty, we can keep one central belief at the forefront: YOU are worthy of physical and emotional health throughout your motherhood journey.

Dismantling these deeply ingrained beliefs and examining their origins, usefulness, and authenticity can be a challenging task. Motherhood often prompts us to scrutinize ourselves from a fresh perspective. During this introspective journey, the support of a therapist can be incredibly beneficial. They can guide you to delve into how your beliefs mold your perceptions and experiences. They can help you understand how both positive and negative experiences have influenced you, and how they impact your mental health. With their assistance, you can devise practical and emotional strategies for this new phase of your life. This therapeutic support could take the form of regular therapy sessions or more condensed coaching sessions focused on creating a postpartum plan. Having professional guidance can help you navigate the complex terrain of motherhood with a clearer understanding and better preparation.

"WE HAVE SEASONS OF GIVING AND SEASONS OF RECEIVING... AS A NEW MOM, YOU ARE IN THE SEASON OF RECEIVING."
-BIRDIE GUNYON MEYER, RN, MA

CHAPTER FIVE

NURTURING SUCCESS IN YOUR TRANSITION INTO MOTHERHOOD:

Having Fulfilling T.A.L.K.S.

Having Fulfilling T.A.L.K.S.

An important factor to you feeling like a "fulfilled mama" is having fulfilling relationships with those around you. One of the most important keys to happy, healthy, and fulfilling relationships is communication. We have broken down the most important keys to healthy communication below because you deserve to have Fulfilling T.A.L.K.S. with all the important people in your life.

T   **Types and Styles of Communication**

A   **Awareness of Self and Others**

L   **Listening actively**

K   **Kindness in Communication**

S   **Silence & Non-Verbal Signals**

Styles of Communication

Communication is a two way street! That means it is not just about your communication style but that of the person you're communicating with. Knowing these communication styles can help you best get your message across and feel heard. Let's discuss different communication styles: passive, aggressive, passive-aggressive, and assertive. We may all engage in some of each but it has been found the assertive communication is best for clear and healthy communication. Below we will break down information about each and tips for how to be more assertive in communication.

COMMUNICATION STYLES

PASSIVE

- Difficulty expressing feelings, ideas, or needs
- Avoidance of confrontation
- Going along with others, even at personal expense
- Frustration when not being heard, despite not speaking up

AGGRESSIVE

- Desire to control conversations
- Disregard for others' input
- Unrealistic demands
- Tendency to overpower others in communication

PASSIVE-AGGRESSIVE

- Avoidance of conflict
- Denial of feelings when asked
- Frequent use of sarcasm
- Stubbornness to prove a point

ASSERTIVE

- Are confident in their needs
- Use "I" statements when expressing their emotions
- Are direct not aggressive
- Remain calm during discussions
- Are understanding of other's needs, opinions, and feelings

Awareness of Self and Others

Communication is the key to happy relationships. It is how we express our thoughts, ideas, and emotions, and how we understand those of others. However, effective communication extends beyond the mere exchange of words. It requires a deep awareness of our own communication patterns as well as those of the people around us.

1. How would you describe your communication style? Are you direct and to-the-point, or do you prefer to communicate in a more subtle, nuanced way?

2. Consider the different people in your life – your family, friends, colleagues. What are their communication styles? How do they differ from yours?

3. Have you ever had to adapt your communication style to better relate to someone else's? Reflect on that experience.

4. Is the way you communicate with others similar to how you like them to communicate with you?

Listening Actively

When we actively listen, we engage fully, eliminating distractions and focusing on the speaker. We interpret their body language, maintain eye contact, and respond appropriately to show them that we genuinely understand and care about their feelings and needs. This kind of engagement is vital in building strong, trusting relationships with our loved ones.

Remember, active listening is not about problem-solving or offering advice—it's about providing a safe space for someone to express themselves without fear of judgment or criticism.

In the midst of the stress of bringing home a new baby, it can be hard to find the time to fully focus on the conversation. We recommend for new parents and those who are intimately involved in the day to day of the household to set aside a check in time every day. This does not have to be long but it is a consistent time when you can give your full attention to one another. That level of focus and attention not only allows you to communicate more effectively but it also lets the other person know you care and value that time together.

How do you and your loved ones connect now? Do you have dedicated time set aside for one another?

Kindness in Communication

In the world of motherhood, where every day can feel like a whirlwind of responsibilities, it's easy to forget the power of kindness in communication. Yet, it's one of the most effective ways to foster understanding, trust, and mutual respect. It's not just about what we say, but how we say it.

Kindness in communication is about expressing ourselves in a way that shows consideration for the other person's feelings. It's listening with empathy, responding with care, and always striving to understand before being understood. This gentle approach can diffuse tension, promote open dialogue, and build stronger relationships.

For new parents navigating the challenges and changes of parenthood, kindness in communication is particularly meaningful. A kind word, an understanding nod, a patient ear — these simple gestures can make a world of difference. They can provide comfort during trying times, remind us that we're not alone, and strengthen our resilience.

1 What is a way you and your loved ones can show kindness to one another in communication?

2 How do you and your loved ones forgive one another after an unkind conversation?

Silence & Non-Verbal Signals

When we think of communication, we often think of verbal communication like an in person conversation between people. We can communicate our emotions, needs, and affection with words.

Verbal Communication:
in person conversation
phone conversations
social media videos
Facetime video

Written Communication:
text message
blogs/websites
emails

As we all know from our day to day life, that is not the only way we communicate with the people in our life. Communication can be body language, with shows of affection through gifts or time spent with one another, or even with lack of speech. Let's break down some common ways we communicate with one another.

Nonverbal Communication:
turning away
eye contact
crossing arms
smiling
silence

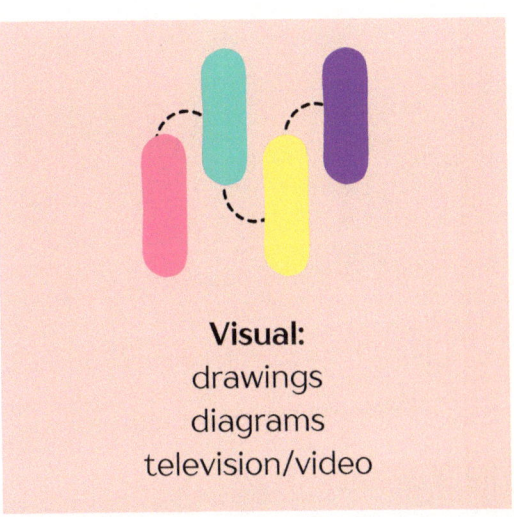

Visual:
drawings
diagrams
television/video

Nonverbal communication can express so many things: anger, happiness, disappointment, a desire for connection, affection, etc.

Common Non-Verbal Communication

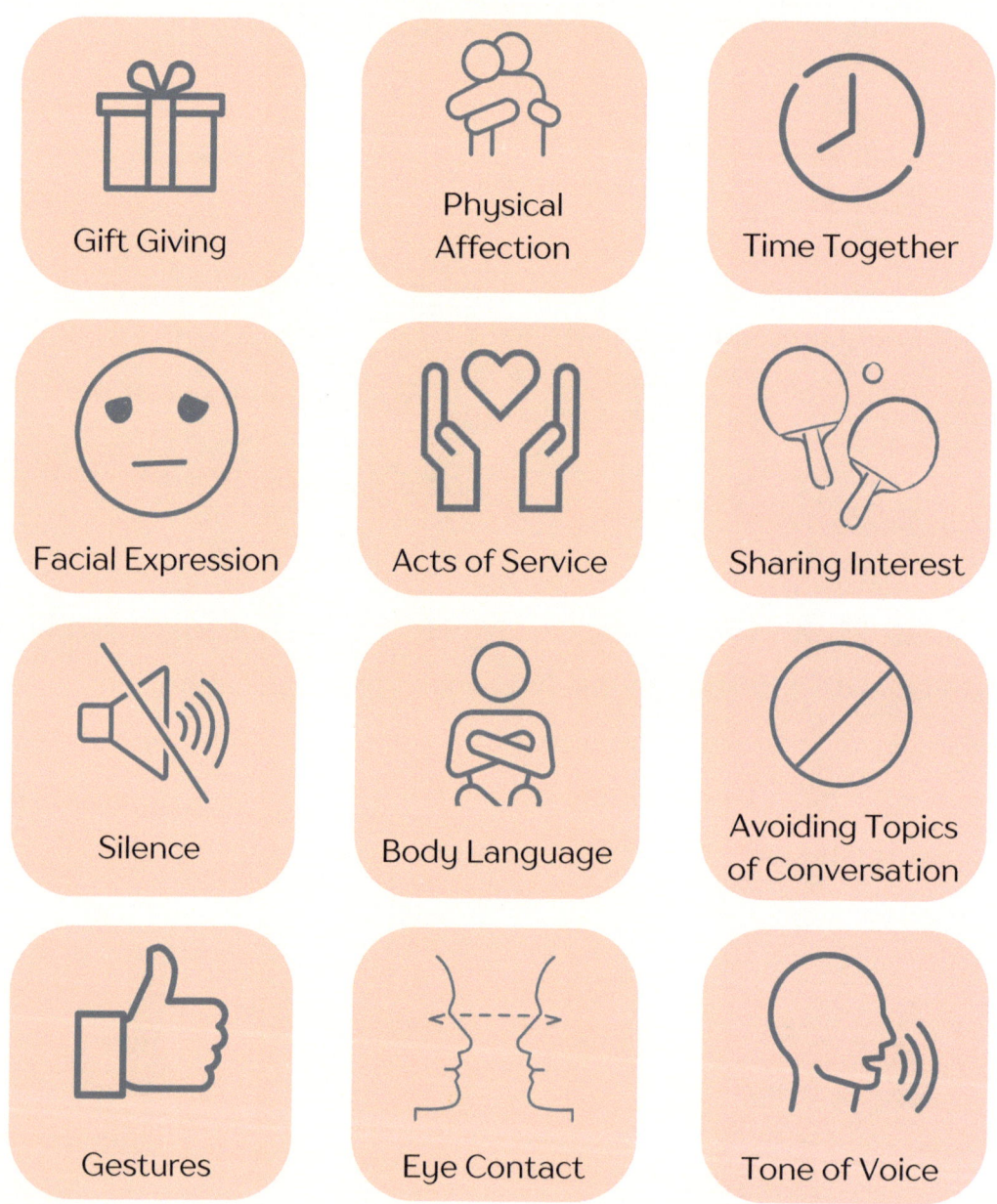

An individual's communication is complex and unique to every person, situation, and relationship. We will be diving into more detail about how we communicate verbally and nonverbally in a future chapter (Beyond the Baby Bump).

Nurturing Success in Your Transition into Motherhood

Let's take a moment to reflect

1 Reflecting on a relationship in your life, what are some differences in your communication?

2 Are there areas of the T.A.L.K.S. framework that you think you could benefit from focusing on?

3 What are some nonverbal ways you communicate with your loved ones? What are some ways they communicate with you?

4 Does your communication style change depending on factors like who you're talking to, your stress level, or the environment? How so?

"GOOD COMMUNICATION
IS THE BRIDGE BETWEEN
CONFUSION AND
CLARITY."
-NAT TURNER

CHAPTER SIX

A MODERN APPROACH TO BALANCED PARENTHOOD:

The Valuable Role of Non-Birthing Parents

Just as every mother is unique, every family is unique. With a variety of family structures, we see a shift and growth in the roles each parent plays and a change in what is expected of each parent based on gender. In this chapter we will be discussing modern fatherhood and the rise of "Rad Dads", non-birthing parents, LGBTQIA+ families, the uniqueness of every family structures, and the way gender affects our view of parenthood.

Since there is limited research on the mental health implication in the postpartum period for parents outside of the heteronormative context, we must make some assumptions. We know that all individuals who become parents are impacted by that transition and all benefit from the opportunity to explore what this role means for them and to seek support for mental health challenges.

Throughout this chapter, we will explore the beliefs and pre-conceived notions we come to parenthood with and the impact that has on the parents we become. By taking a few moments to explore our own beliefs and expectations about ourselves, our role as caregivers, and what that means for our future as parents, you can step into this new role with the confidence you deserve. Although we utilize word "parent" throughout this chapter, we recognize that there are limitless family structures and individuals who serve as parent figures in the lives of children. To all who step into that role, this is for you.

For a quick refresher on how we can explore and question our pre-conceived notions and automatic thoughts, take a look back at page 33. We can utilize this same framework as we explore our expectations around parenthood:

Modern Fatherhood

In line with the transformation of motherhood, the roles of fathers is also undergoing a significant evolution. This shift has given rise to the "Rad Dad" phenomenon – fathers who fully embrace their parenting role, viewing themselves as equal co-parents, not secondary figures in their children's lives. Rad Dads are redefining the norm, willing to adopt modern roles such as being stay-at-home dads, actively participating in household chores, and taking on parenting responsibilities more intensively than previous generations. In internalizing this title of Rad Dad, dads in person and online are creating a shift the way fathers show up in parenting and how they support one another.

While this progressive shift promises substantial benefits for their children and families, societal norms are still in the process of catching up. Like we have discussed in previous chapters of this book, so much of our beliefs around parenthood come from our own experiences, society, and understood norms of our community. To all the Rad Dads out there, we see you, we stand by you, and are thrilled to support your journey into evolved fatherhood! This pursuit of a new view of fatherhood allows you to enter this role with confidence, authenticity, and the ability to embrace what makes you unique.

Challenges Faced by Modern Fathers

Let's talk about the challenges faced by our Rad Dads. As these fathers are changing the societal norm surrounding what fatherhood can look like, they are often left with limited support and a challenge of their masculinity.

While we will delve into the statistics surrounding perinatal mood disorders in mothers in a subsequent chapter, it's crucial to address the prevalence of these conditions among fathers. Indeed, fathers can and frequently do encounter perinatal mood disorders such as depression, anxiety, or OCD during their partner's pregnancy or in the postpartum period.

10%

of fathers will experience a perinatal mood disorder

Despite this considerable prevalence, there is a noticeable scarcity of outreach programs, screening protocols, and resources tailored specifically for fathers in need of support.

Compounding this issue is the societal stigma associated with mens' mental health, which often discourages men from seeking help. This can result in detrimental coping mechanisms, such as increased alcohol dependence, withdrawal from family interactions, and other non-constructive behaviors.

We firmly believe that Rad Dads deserve emotional support during this significant life transition, equal to the support offered to mothers. In many instances, Rad Dads are so focused on supporting their partners that they may feel their needs are overlooked or sidelined. Recognizing this, it becomes evident that implementing a comprehensive support strategy is vital – one that caters not only to the mother and baby but also to the father.

A Modern Approach to Balanced Parenthood

What is Flexible Masculinity?

Flexible masculinity is the idea that there's no universal definition of what it means to be a man or a father. We're leaving behind the stereotypical notions of what a man 'should be' and celebrating each individual for who they truly are. Similar to our previous discussions on values and boundaries, let's explore what masculinity signifies to you, both as an individual and a father.

1 Consider what "masculinity" means to you. Write down your definitions, thoughts, or ideas. Remember, there are no wrong answers. This exercise is about understanding your perspective.

Reflect on how your definitions or thoughts resonate with you. Traditional masculinity can sometimes feel constraining or limiting. By redefining this concept, we can enhance mental health outcomes for fathers and enable a more genuine expression of self.

Let's momentarily shift away from the topic of masculinity.

2 What makes you feel fulfilled, content, or happy?

Do your personal definitions of masculinity align with what brings you joy and satisfaction? Let's contemplate how you could broaden your perception of masculinity. Utilizing the belief exploration framework can be helpful.

3 Think about how you might broaden your definition of masculinity. What traits or behaviors would you add?

4 How might these additions make you feel more comfortable in your role as a father?

Remember, everyone's journey with flexible masculinity and fatherhood is unique. The objective of this exercise is to assist you in defining and understanding these concepts for yourself. As you navigate through these activities, know that you're taking a crucial step towards embracing your personalized version of balanced parenthood.

A Modern Approach to Balanced Parenthood

Balanced Parenthood in LGBTQIA+ Families

Welcoming a new life into your family is a joyous occasion, but it can also present unique challenges and stresses for non-birthing parents. It's essential to recognize that the mental health of non-birthing parents is just as important as that of birthing parents during the perinatal period.

Contrary to popular belief, mental health concerns such as perinatal depression and anxiety aren't exclusive to birthing mothers. As discussed in the previous section about dads, research indicates that between 5-10% of fathers experience perinatal depression and 5–15% experience perinatal anxiety. These experiences are not limited to heterosexual couples; they're increasingly recognized within LGBTQIA+ communities and amongst other non-birthing parents

The transition to parenthood can be emotionally charged and stressful for anyone, especially when compounded by additional pressures like work stress, financial worries, or past mental health issues. Non-birthing parents might also worry about forming a bond with the baby or feel overwhelmed by the increased responsibility. Research has shown a few common concerns within LGBTQIA+ non-birthing parents: *A Question of Recognition, An Insecure Connection,* and *Carving Your Way* as we will continue to discuss in this chapter.

It's worth noting that postpartum depression in dads and co-parents is more likely if the birthing parent is also experiencing depression. If one partner is facing emotional or mental health difficulties, it can heighten the risk for the other.

No matter your role in the parenting journey, it's important to take care of your mental health. You're not alone in your experiences, and acknowledging your feelings is the first step towards finding support and fostering a healthy environment for your growing family.

An important first step in any journey of parenthood is reflecting on your own beliefs and expectations surrounding your role, what you bring to parenthood, and what that means for you.

Challenges Faced by LGBTQIA+ Non-Birthing Parents

Although every family and relationship is unique, a few common themes have come up when non-birthing parents were polled about their parenting concerns: *A Question of Recognition, An Insecure Connection,* and *Carving Your Way.* Let's break down what each of these concerns may mean for you.

A Question of Recognition
For many non-birthing parents, there is a question of how others will recognize them as a parent and also how they will identify as a parent. This can look like anything from decisions about legal adoption if needed to what your name will be as a parent. Our desire to be recognized and connected to our child is universal. Like so many things in life, how you decide to identify that role and that title is up to you.

In Insecure Connection
Like many non-birthing parents, you may wonder about what your connection or bond with your baby will look like compared to that of the birthing mother. This is such an important topic to explore within yourself and within your relationship. What are those things that help you feel bonded and connected with someone? What do you image that role as a parent to look like? Thinking about your own family of origin, what are those things that made your family feel like a family unit?

Carving Your Own Way
Becoming a parent is challenging enough without the struggle to find other parents who are walking your same path. Being able to see others going through similar experiences can be comforting and a source of support. When your family looks a little different than others in your immediate community, it can be harder to find people to turn to who have the same experiences as you. There can be benefit in seeking connection even virtually with other non-birthing parents and seeking out support of professionals who have supported non-birthing parents before. You can create your own path but it is often comforting to be able to turn to others who have been down the path before.

LGBTQIA+ Families and Non-Birthing Parents

It can be challenging to know your role and expectations when there is so much focus on the baby and birthing parent. Let's explore your personal identity and expectations of parenthood together.

1 Consider what your role as parent means to you. Where does this image of parenthood come from?

Reflect on how your definitions or thoughts resonate with you. Traditional views of gender and roles can sometimes feel constraining or limiting especially when we think about roles of parenthood. By redefining this concept, we can enhance mental health outcomes for parents and enable a more genuine expression of self. Let's take a moment to shift away from gender and focus on you.

2 What makes you feel fulfilled, content, or happy? What values are important to you?

Do your personal definitions of your gender, parenthood and personal identity align with what brings you joy and satisfaction? Let's contemplate how you could broaden your perception of what your role as a parent means to you.

3 Think about how you might broaden your definition. What traits or behaviors would you add?

4 How might these additions make you feel more comfortable in or impact your role as a parent?

Remember, everyone's journey with gender expectations and parenthood is unique. The objective of this exercise is to assist you in defining and understanding these concepts for yourself. As you navigate through these activities, know that you're taking a crucial step towards embracing your personalized version of balanced parenthood.

Overcoming Maternal Gatekeeping for Balanced Parenting

Moms, it's time for a heart-to-heart. A common challenge you may encounter upon entering motherhood is the tendency to gatekeep. You might feel an overwhelming sense that you alone know best, insisting on doing things your way. While this can be a normal response, it can also signal underlying anxiety or OCD (we'll delve deeper into this later).

But here's the thing – with the rise of equality in parenthood, it's time to let go of the notion that you need to shoulder everything because "You're the mom". This shift requires a conscious effort and work, but if you want your partner to fully embrace their role, it's crucial to start dismantling those 'gates' during pregnancy. This is an opportunity to explore this belief around moms having to do it all and let your partner step into their role too!

We understand that as a mom, you want the best for your child and so does your partner! Involving your partner in the decision-making process is a powerful way to ensure this. Encourage them to take part in choosing baby items, researching birth classes, pediatricians, and lactation consultants. Believe us when we say they're ready and willing to be an active participant!

The rise of the equality in parenthood is a positive shift towards shared parenting responsibilities, and it goes hand-in-hand with reducing maternal gatekeeping. By empowering your partner to embrace their role, their potential to contribute significantly to your child's upbringing shines brightly. Now, let's make a plan to support this journey!

Let's dive into some activities to help you create a supportive environment for partner.

1 How do you envision splitting the role of parenting? List these down and discuss them together.

2 How can you ensure that you and your partner feel included and valued in the decision-making process related to your child's upbringing?

3 Are there any parenting tasks or decisions that you may have a hard time sharing with your partner?

A Modern Approach to Balanced Parenthood

4 How can you communicate effectively about parenting responsibilities without falling into the pattern of 'gatekeeping'?

5 Think about how you can show appreciation for your partner's efforts in parenting. What are some ways you can express this appreciation? What are some ways you would like to be shown appreciation?

Remember, the path to becoming a partnership isn't a sprint; it's a marathon. It requires patience, understanding, and consistent effort from both parents. But rest assured, every step you take is a stride towards creating a nurturing environment for your child and a stronger bond within your family.

As we wrap up this chapter, we hope you feel equipped with the tools and knowledge needed to navigate the exciting terrain of co-parenting. Remember, your efforts today are shaping the Rad Dads, empowered parents, and families of tomorrow.

"BE THE PARENT TODAY
THAT YOU WANT YOUR
KIDS TO REMEMBER
TOMORROW."

CHAPTER SEVEN

BEYOND THE BABY BUMP:

Nurturing Marriage and Relationship

Navigating the journey of motherhood can bring about profound changes, and your relationship with your significant other is no exception. You're not alone if you find your partnership facing new challenges in the postpartum period. Please remember, these challenges aren't permanent, but part of the evolving landscape of your shared life.

Much like the transformation you experience as a mother, your relationship too can evolve, emerging stronger and more resilient. Your union is an integral thread in the fabric of your family and it deserves to be nurtured with the same level of care. Let's talk about why relationships go through periods of change in the postpartum period.

Understanding the Changes

Becoming a parent is a transformative experience filled with a spectrum of emotions and a multitude of changes. As you navigate this new chapter of life, it's important to recognize and understand the impact it can have on your relationship with your significant other.

The emotional journey post-childbirth is a complex one. Euphoria, anxiety, exhaustion, and love all intertwine, creating a whirlwind of feelings that can be overwhelming. These intense emotions may sometimes cloud your interactions with your partner, leading to misunderstandings or conflict. But remember, it's completely normal to experience these emotional highs and lows.

Physically, the postpartum period can be challenging as well. Your body is healing and adapting to no longer being pregnant, which can take time and patience. This physical transformation might affect intimacy in your relationship, but it's crucial to remember that every woman's journey is unique and there's no 'right' timeline for resuming physical closeness. Open communication about your physical comfort and needs can help foster understanding between you and your partner during this time.

Lastly, lifestyle changes are inevitable after the arrival of a child. Your routine is now punctuated by diaper changes, feedings, and nap times. The added responsibilities can leave less room for couple time. However, incorporating small moments of connection, like a shared glance during your baby's adorable antics or a quick hug in between chores, can help keep the spark alive.

Remember, change is a part of life, especially when you're stepping into parenthood. These changes can feel monumental, but with understanding, communication, and a help from professionals like your physician or a therapist if needed, you can navigate them successfully. Every challenge faced together can become an opportunity to strengthen your relationship and deepen your bond.

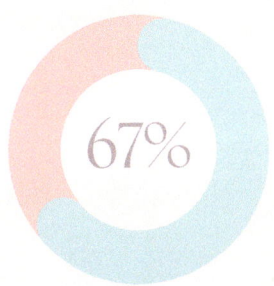

67% of couples report feeling less content in their relationship following the birth of their first child

A study by psychotherapist and marriage researcher John Gottman revealed that an overwhelming 67% of couples experienced a dip in relationship contentment following the birth of their first child. This shift generally manifests around six months for women and nine months for men post the baby's arrival. That number may be shocking or scary, but I want you to take comfort in knowing this difficult period in relationships is normal and can be overcome.

Communication is Key

As you may remember from our previous chapter on having Fulfilling T.A.L.K.S., there are many factors to keep in mind when we are striving for healthy communication with our loved ones. Let's take a look at how each of these factors could impact a romantic relationship.

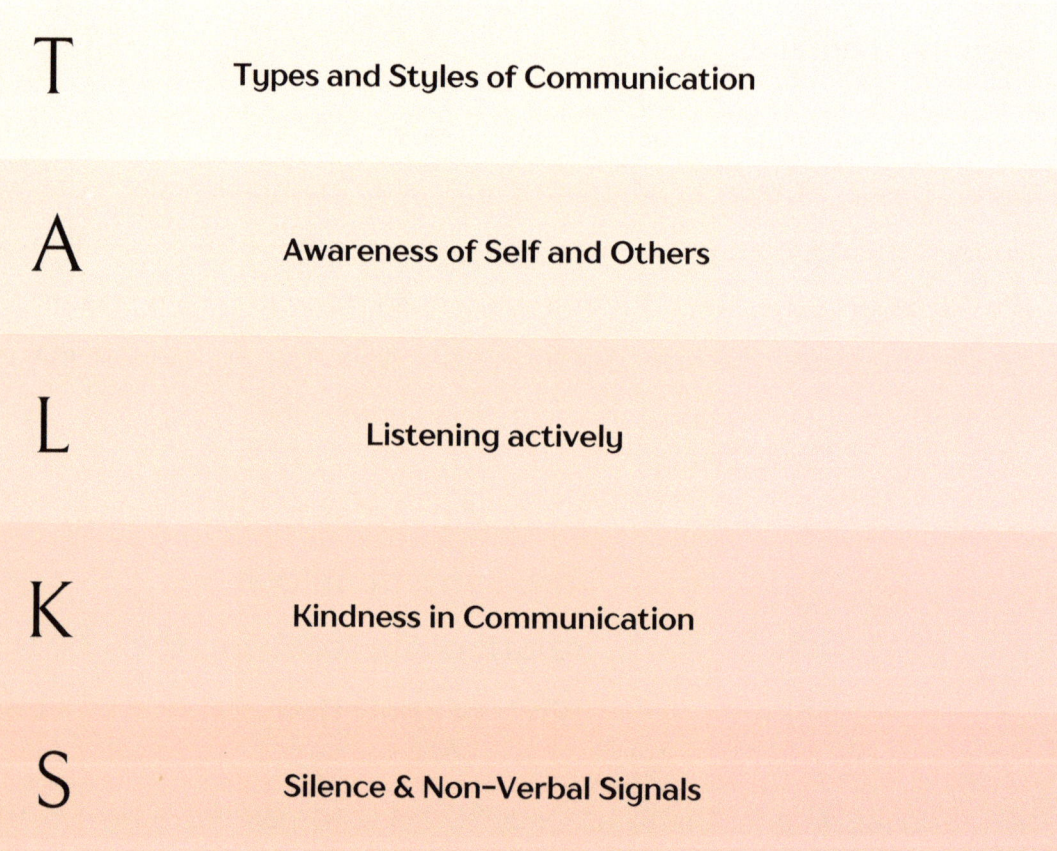

T — **Types and Styles of Communication**

A — **Awareness of Self and Others**

L — **Listening actively**

K — **Kindness in Communication**

S — **Silence & Non-Verbal Signals**

Let's break it down together.

Beyond the Baby Bump

Styles of Communication

PASSIVE
- Difficulty expressing feelings, ideas, or needs
- Avoidance of confrontation
- Going along with others, even at personal expense
- Frustration when not being heard, despite not speaking up

AGGRESSIVE
- Desire to control conversations
- Disregard for others' input
- Unrealistic demands
- Tendency to overpower others in communication

PASSIVE-AGGRESSIVE
- Avoidance of conflict
- Denial of feelings when asked
- Frequent use of sarcasm
- Stubbornness to prove a point

ASSERTIVE
- Are confident in their needs
- Use "I" statements when expressing their emotions
- Are direct not aggressive
- Remain calm during discussions
- Are understanding of other's needs, opinions, and feelings

1 How do each of these communication styles look like in your relationship?

2 Are there situations in which you utilize each of these communication styles more?

Awareness of Self and Others

In every relationship, distinct patterns of communication naturally emerge, shaping the unique rhythm and tone of our interactions. As partners, we often intuitively become attuned to each other's characteristic ways of expressing thoughts and feelings, even if we are not consciously aware of it.

1   How do you and your significant other have difficult conversations with one another? Do you each have a different preference?

2   What makes each of you feel heard and understood?

3   What normally causes disagreements between you?

4   Do you and your partner prefer talking about issues in the moment or after the fact?

Listening Actively

Win the journey of parenthood, active listening becomes an essential tool to maintain and strengthen the bond in your romantic relationship. It involves completely immersing yourself in the conversation, discarding distractions, and focusing on your partner. By observing their body language, maintaining eye contact, and responding thoughtfully, you demonstrate that you genuinely understand and value their feelings and needs. This level of engagement is crucial in fostering trust and deepening connections with your loved ones.

It's important to remember that active listening isn't about providing solutions or advice — it's about creating a judgment-free zone where your partner can express themselves openly.

In the whirlwind of welcoming a new baby, carving out time for focused conversation might seem challenging. Therefore, we encourage new parents, and those deeply involved in the household's routine, to establish a daily check-in time. It doesn't need to be lengthy, but a dedicated time when you can offer your undivided attention to each other. This focus not only facilitates effective communication but also conveys your care and appreciation for these shared moments.

What helps you and your partner feel connected now? What helps when you're feeling emotionally distant or feeling at odds?

Kindness in Communication

In the initial stages of parenthood, the combination of stress, sleep deprivation, and navigating new challenges can sometimes leave couples feeling as though they're barely keeping it together. This strain can often manifest in petty disagreements and misplaced frustrations. However, by acknowledging this reality, we can help you devise a strategy to reconnect with one another, identify when tensions are escalating, and use your plan to foster understanding and unity.

1 What are simple ways you and your significant other show affection and kindness now?

2 How do you and your significant other forgive one another after an unkind conversation?

3 We encourage you to brainstorm together a list of simple things that help each of you feel love and kindness from one another. These can be a reminder of how to be kind to one another in trying times.

Silence & Non-Verbal Signals

Nonverbal communication can express so many things: anger, happiness, disappointment, a desire for connection, affection, etc. Below are a few examples.

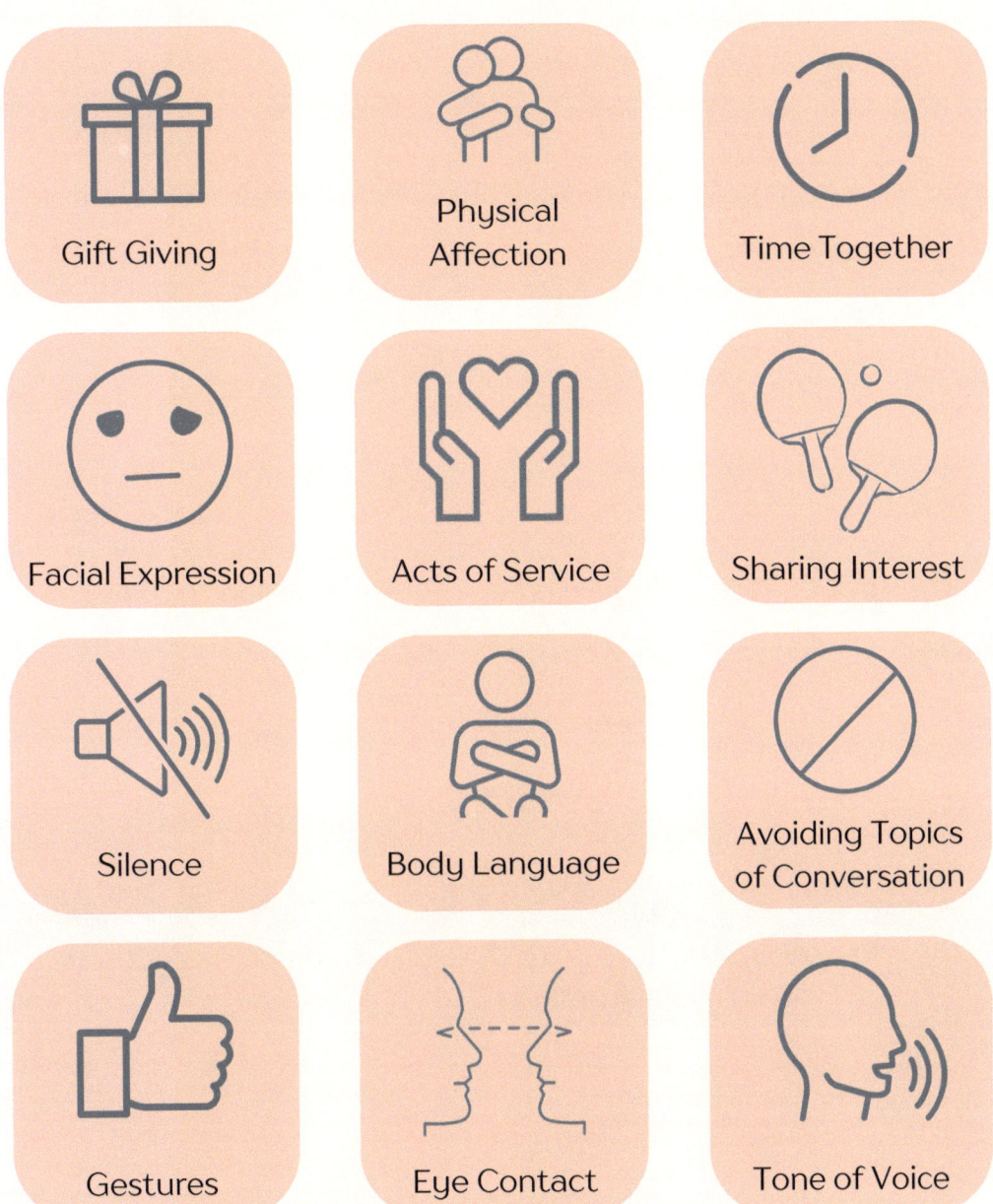

Gift Giving

Physical Affection

Time Together

Facial Expression

Acts of Service

Sharing Interest

Silence

Body Language

Avoiding Topics of Conversation

Gestures

Eye Contact

Tone of Voice

Let's take a moment to reflect

1 Utilizing the examples above how do you communicate your emotions to your partner?

2 How do you like to receive affection and shows of love from your partner?

3 How does your spouse communicate emotions to you?

4 How does your significant other like to receive affection and shows of love from you?

Intimacy After Baby

Becoming a parent is a life-changing event that ushers in a new chapter of growth, love, and discovery. However, it can also introduce challenges in maintaining intimacy with your partner. This shift often occurs as the focus naturally gravitates towards the care and nurture of your newborn. It's essential to know that this experience is shared by many new parents—it's completely normal and part of the journey of parenthood.

Intimacy after childbirth may look different for every couple—there's no standard 'right' approach. What's important is fostering an environment of open communication where both partners feel safe expressing their feelings, needs, and concerns. This could involve setting aside regular 'couple time', discussing physical comfort levels, or finding new ways to express affection.

Remember, rekindling intimacy post-baby isn't just about physical connection—it's also about emotional closeness, understanding, and mutual support. It's about navigating this journey together, hand in hand, with patience and love. With the right support and resources, these initial challenges can transition into opportunities for deepening your bond and strengthening your partnership, creating a foundation of love and support for your growing family.

What is intimacy?

When many think of intimacy after having a baby, their first thought is sex after baby. While sex is definitely a form of intimacy, it is not the only thing that can create intimacy in a relationship. Think back to when you first started dating your partner. What were some of those subtle intimate moments that brought you closer together? Those could be shared laughs, physical touch, or shared memories.

> What is your definition of intimacy in your relationship?

Silence & Non-Verbal Signals

There are several kinds of intimacy:

Emotional Intimacy: This involves a deep sense of understanding and mutual respect between partners, where feelings, thoughts, and fears can be shared openly without judgment.

Intellectual Intimacy: This form of intimacy is built on mutual respect for each other's minds, where partners can engage in stimulating discussions, share ideas, and challenge each other intellectually.

Physical Intimacy: Beyond sexual activity, physical intimacy includes any form of touch that brings comfort and closeness, like hand-holding, hugging, or simply sitting close to each other.

Experiential Intimacy: This involves shared experiences or activities that create a bond between partners. This could include hobbies, travel, or simply spending quality time together.

Spiritual Intimacy: This type of intimacy is about sharing a common set of values or beliefs, which can strengthen the bond between partners by providing a shared perspective on life and its challenges.

Creative Intimacy: This involves sharing and appreciating each other's creative expressions, such as art, music, writing, cooking, or any form of creativity that allows partners to connect on a deeper level.

Communication Intimacy: This refers to the ability to talk openly about anything, expressing thoughts and feelings honestly and clearly, creating an atmosphere of trust and mutual understanding.

Can you think of an example of each of these in your relationship currently? This can be examples of intimacy you like and examples of what your partner likes.

Emotional Intimacy

Intellectual Intimacy

Physical Intimacy

Experiential Intimacy

Spiritual Intimacy

Creative Intimacy

Communication Intimacy

Factors Impacting Intimacy After Baby

Several factors can impact intimacy after the arrival of a baby. Hormonal changes, physical discomfort, exhaustion, and the demands of caring for a newborn can all contribute to a decreased desire for intimacy. It's important to remember that these experiences are completely normal and part of the transition into parenthood.

Communication plays a crucial role in navigating these changes. Openly discussing your feelings, concerns, and physical comfort levels with your partner can foster understanding and mutual support. This might also involve exploring new ways to express love and affection, or establishing 'couple time' to reconnect on a physical level.

Remember, there's no set timeline or 'right' way to resume physical intimacy post-baby. Every couple's journey is unique; and patience, understanding, and open communication are key. If you and your significant other are both ready for and open to physical intimacy but it is feeling uncomfortable or painful physically, we strongly encourage you to reach out to your physician for support. There is medical support and care available to you that can help make physical intimacy comfortable. For all postpartum couples, we encourage utilizing lubrication as needed due to common hormonal changes following childbirth.

In the following sections we'll take a look at how you can work together as a couple to maintain room for your relationship in the midst of this major life change.

Remember, every couple and every relationship is different. There is no normal or correct timeline in which to resume sexual activity.

Sharing Responsibilities

Nothing puts a damper on a relationship quite like the stress of managing a home. With a baby involved, the tasks around your home seem to grow exponentially. By taking time now to put all of these tasks on the table without judgement, you can create a plan that leaves you both feeling supported, accomplished, and affectionate toward one another as equal partners.

Eve Rodsky, the author of the book Fair Play, has done immense work exploring how couples communicate about and balance the day to day tasks of the home. The Fair Play system is a revolutionary approach designed to foster balance, peace, and shared responsibility within households. It's centered around understanding and redistributing domestic tasks in a fair manner, not necessarily equally, between partners. This method is not just about housework; it's about redefining expectations, minimizing resentment, and creating a more balanced partnership.

The Fair Play concept is straightforward yet profoundly impactful. It involves the use of a figurative deck of cards, each representing a different household task. The idea is for couples to go through this deck together, discussing each task and deciding who should take responsibility for it. This process helps to clearly define roles and responsibilities, reducing ambiguity and potential conflicts.

What's unique about Fair Play is that it's not just about dividing tasks, but also about acknowledging and appreciating the invisible work often undertaken by mothers. It explores gender inequality in the division of domestic labor and its impact on mental health, particularly for women. Ultimately, Eve Rodsky's Fair Play is more than a method; it's a philosophy that promotes respect, understanding, and fairness within domestic partnerships.

Finding Time for Each Other

Before baby, finding time for one another is probably not too difficult. It may take some planning but date nights and special time together happen. You may find that in the postpartum period this doesn't feel as easy. This doesn't mean time together is impossible. It just takes some creativity. This is where regular check ins, dates at home, scheduling regular dates as support allows, and finding opportunities for connection come in.

1 What helps you and your significant other feel connected now? Are there activities you do together regularly?

2 Take a few moments to brainstorm with your partner ways you can connect with one another including small moments of connect, home date nights, and if possible a regular date night out of the house.

3 Talk to your partner about choosing a time every day to check in with one another. During that time you can explore if there are ways you can better love one another, any disagreements that came up, and share moments of intimacy.

4 What is the minimum you need each day to feel intimate and connected? What about your partner?

"LIFE IS A CRAZY RIDE. IT'S A PRIVILEGE TO GO THROUGH IT WITH A PARTNER."
-KRISTEN BELL

CHAPTER EIGHT

NURTURING YOURSELF AND PRACTICAL PREPARATION:

Prioritizing Rest, Nutrition, and Support

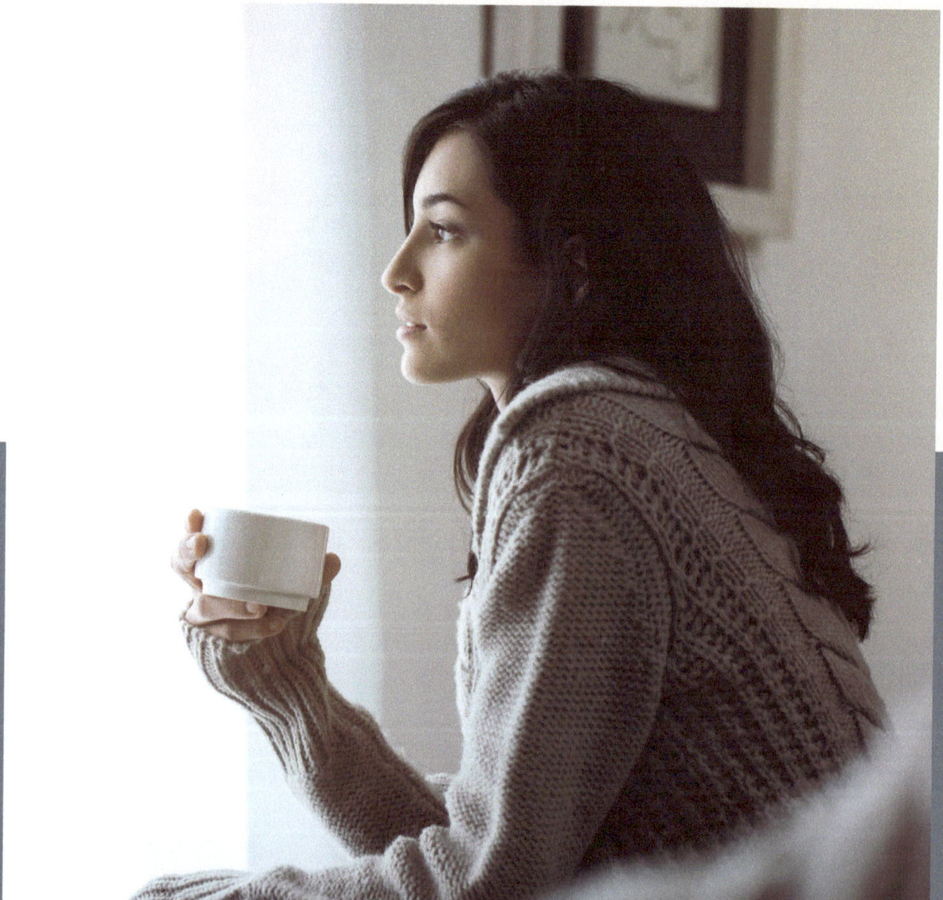

Section One – Navigating the Sleep Conundrum: Plans, Myths and Impacts

Motherhood is a journey filled with joy and challenges. One of the significant hurdles new moms face is dealing with sleep deprivation. This chapter will explore how to tackle this issue effectively, debunk common myths and provide practical sleep plan examples.

Sleep deprivation can lead to several physical and emotional impacts:

1. Irritability, anger, and rage
2. Increased anxiety
3. Lower mood or depression
4. Slower reaction times, leading to potential accidents or injuries
5. Brain fog
6. Higher levels of stress
7. Difficulty regulating emotions
8. Lesser ability to cope with daily challenges
9. Decreased patience, increased reactivity, and irritability

Understanding these impacts underscores the importance of managing sleep effectively for new mothers.

We all know that some sleepless nights come with parenthood, but that doesn't mean we can't plan for your body to receive the rest and care it needs. In this next section, we'll break down some common myths surrounding motherhood and sleep as well as some tips for getting the sleep your body needs. Remember, even the best mother is a human. Humans needs sleep and that includes you.

Myths about Motherhood and Sleep

1. It's solely the mom's responsibility to get up with the baby.
2. If nursing, no one else can help with the baby overnight.
3. Moms should be selfless and sacrifice their sleep for the baby.
4. The working parent's sleep should be protected at all costs.
5. Moms have a special ability to settle their baby at night and should be the one getting up with them.
6. Asking for help signifies an inability to handle motherhood.

Truths about Motherhood and Sleep

1. Overnight responsibility can be shared.
2. If mom is nursing, she can be supported by changing baby's diaper, resettling, and getting baby back to sleep so she only has to wake for feeds.
3. Moms require sleep to function.
4. Families can be creative to find ways to protect sleep for both parents.
5. Parents are both learning and will each develop ways to soothe their baby.
6. Asking for help shows you want to best for yourself and your family. It allows you to opportunity to be supported.

Planning for Effective Sleep

While newborn sleep patterns may be unpredictable, there are aspects of the mother's sleep that can be controlled:

1. Research shows that an uninterrupted 4-5 hours of sleep is needed for the body to complete full sleep cycles and have restorative sleep.
2. Prioritize chunks of uninterrupted sleep and supplement with naps when possible.
3. Utilize support from others (significant other, mother, sister, or paid postpartum doula) to aim for that uninterrupted chunk of sleep.
4. Utilize healthy sleep hygiene to promote the best sleep possible when you do go to sleep- sleep in a dark room, minimize your caffeine if possible, and limit the use of screens.

Overnight Care

- There are many ways to support one another in overnight care.
    - taking "shifts" to allow longer stretches of sleep
    - for breastfeeding moms, this can be a challenge at times and may benefit from a teamwork approach. The non-breastfeeding partner can help settle the baby, change the baby, and get them back to sleep once mom has nursed.
    - For pumping moms, this may look like taking shifts but only getting up during your "sleeping time" to pump while letting the other partner do the rest of the care.
    - For families utilizing formula, alternating between feeds In the middle of the night, or taking chunks of time (ie 11pm-2am, 3am-6am) to allow each partner to get restorative sleep
- Things to consider when making your own overnight care schedule:
    - Schedules for the next day
    - Feeding preferences
    - Aiming for 5-6 hour sleep stretches for each parent
    - How the parent who is not feeding can support the feeding parent
        - Setting up for the next diaper change
        - Preparing the swaddle for after the feed
        - Getting a nursing mom snacks, water, etc.
        - Setting up mom's breast pump, if applicable
        - Washing bottles, if needed

Next we will walk through a sample overnight schedule. There will be a blank overnight schedule In our worksheets section that you can fill In your own schedule and/or use to plan.

SAMPLE OVERNIGHT ROUTINE
Nursing Mom Edition

7 pm	Mom nurses baby and put down for longest stretch of sleep
8 pm	Mom goes to sleep
9 pm	
10 pm	Partner gives bottle of previously pumped breastmilk or formula
11 pm	Partner goes to sleep
12 am	
1 am	Mom nurses baby, partner sleeps through to get a good stretch of sleep
2 am	
3 am	
4 am	Mom nurses baby, partner assists with diapering, readying baby's space to go back to sleep
5 am	
6 am	
7 am	Family is up for the day

Nurturing Yourself and Practical Preparation

In reflecting on our own postpartum experiences and those of the many moms we have worked with, we compiled a list of top tips we want you to know to help you prepare for a confident and supported postpartum period. These includes tips to help prepare your home, food prep, make things easier for yourself postpartum, get the rest you need, allow those around you to help you, and so much more.

Preparing for Meals

- Plan for at least four week postpartum with nourishing meals that you will enjoy, are easy to freeze, provide well rounded nutrition, and some snacks.

- Never cook for just one meal, if you are going to make a meal, double the recipe so you can freeze part of it to have another day.

- Enlist the help of a meal train! A meal train is an opportunity for individuals to sign up to provide a meal to the new parents. This can be through food delivery, them bringing home cooked meals, or them picking up items you like. It's all your preference!

- Consider waiting to start your meal train until a few weeks postpartum when the initial support often dwindles.

- Communicate your preferences! The last thing you want is the well meaning food delivery to be food you won't enjoy.

- Request things like Door Dash gift cards on your baby registry.

- Utilize paper plates when you can. Your ability to be nourished and rested are important during this time!

- Plan crockpot meals that can be left to slow cook.

- Utilize disposable cookware when you're able to make clean up easier.

Embracing Support: Delegating Tasks and Receiving Help

✳ Create a list of ways people can help you by splitting them into categories based on time commitment when they stop by. We have included a worksheet you can utilize to organize these tasks!

✳ If you're uncomfortable asking friends or family to do specific chores, like cleaning bathrooms, consider budgeting for professional help.

✳ Ask for gifts of time for your baby shower! Request friends and family commit a few hours of time after baby arrives to assist with various chores.

✳ Have a nesting party! Have your friends and family over before baby comes to help prepare the house, to meal prep, and to set you up for success once baby gets here!

✳ Explore if there are members of your support system who would be interested in coming by regularly for an hour or so to give you time to rest, shower, or have time to yourself.

✳ Request things like Door Dash gift cards on your baby registry.

✳ Chore Train: think of a chore train instead of a meal train. While meals are certainly helpful, having people sign up to complete specific chores can be equally beneficial. Create a list of tasks from which they can choose, making it easier for them to offer help in a way that suits them best.

✳ Identify if there is a person in your life you feel comfortable with helping to coordinate the help of your friends, family, and community. It can be uncomfortable asking for help but identifying one person you're comfortable with organizing this effort can make this easier for you.

Visitors

✻ Consider the following if you want visitors at the hospital? Consider the number of visitors permitted to visit. If so, who?

✻ In thinking about your birth preferences, consider how different people in your life could support those preferences. That may help you decide who to have present at the hospital.

✻ Discuss what guidelines you would want your visitors to follow both at the hospital and at home. This can include timing of visits, length of visits, washing hands, holding the baby, calling ahead, or anything else that is important to you.

✻ Discuss if you would we want anyone to stay overnight for support (family, friends, doula)?

✻ Remember that your decisions around visitors postpartum is completely up to you! Create a plan with your significant other or support partner about how to communicate your boundaries around visitors. It can be helpful to identify one person to field questions once you are in labor and postpartum to take that stress off your plate.

✻ Create a plan for who will be informed when you go into labor or when baby is born. How will they be informed?

✻ Consider a sign on the door indicating if you're open to visitors or if baby is sleeping.

Feeding

❀ Discuss preferences surrounding feeding knowing you can change your mind at any point.

❀ If nursing exclusively, the non-nursing partner can help support through things like helping bring snacks and drinks, helping the nursing partner learn how to latch, and supporting in non feeding related ways.

❀ For pumping moms, the non-breastfeeding partner can help with cleaning the bottles and pumping parts while the breastfeeding partner pumps.

❀ If you're interested in breastfeeding, connect with a local lactation consultant during pregnancy for education and to have someone to call postpartum. Even if you decide not to breastfeed, it is better to already have that support in place.

❀ If you're even considering utilizing bottles (formula and breast milk), have a few on hand as well as samples of formula to alleviate that stress of having to coordinate obtaining those items in the moment.

❀ For pumping moms, having multiple sets of pumping parts if possible can help eliminate some of the stress of constantly washing parts.

❀ Nursing bras can be utilized as pumping bras in a pinch.

Supporting One Another

✽ As soon as you feel comfortable, try to create a schedule in which both partners have the opportunity to rest. This can look like each person having a "sleep in" day on a regular basis or picking a time on a regular basis to utilize however you choose.

✽ Agree upon an intentional check in time to reconnect as a couple, problem solve issues that have come up, check in on each other's emotions, and create a plan for any issues that have come up.

✽ When it feels right, schedule a date night with childcare so you can get a little 1:1 time. We realize that this will feel different for everyone, but even a few hours away will make a difference.

✽ Find intimacy outside of the bedroom, think about ways you previously were able to emotionally connect and lean into those as you can.

Working as a Team

✽ Remember that you are in it together!

✽ Many public restroom won't have changing tables in the men's bathrooms. It can be helpful to talk about a plan beforehand.

✽ You can be creative with moments of connection. This could be as simple as a walk as a family to the mailbox or a drive around the box. Use these quiet moments to reconnect as a couple.

✽ Give your spouse kudos for their parenting growth. Everyone is still learning and it feels great to get a heartfelt compliment.

✽ Remember what you love about each other. This can be an anchor during tough times.

"WE SPEND SO MUCH TIME PLANNING FOR LABOR AND DELIVERY, BUT NO ONE PREPARES YOU FOR YOUR BODY OR HEART AFTER YOU LEAVE THE HOSPITAL."

CHAPTER NINE

EMPOWERING YOUR BIRTH EXPERIENCE:

Advocating for Yourself and Your Wellbeing

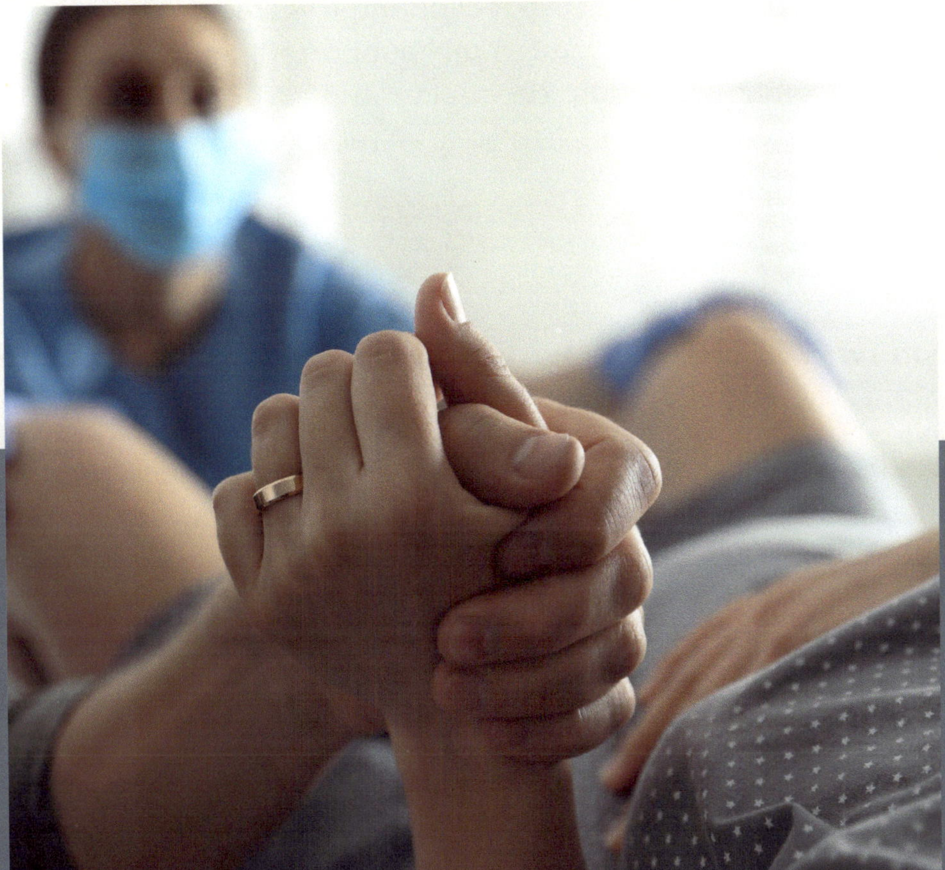

Contrary to popular belief, it is not a matter of choosing between the health of the baby and the health of the mother. Both aspects are equally important and interconnected. While the primary focus is often directed towards ensuring the wellbeing of the baby, it is vital to prioritize the physical, mental, and emotional health of the mother as well. By nurturing and supporting mothers throughout the entire birthing process, we can ensure positive outcomes for both mom and baby.

Section One: Understanding Your Birth Preferences

A birth plan can be a powerful tool that allows you to envision and communicate your desires for the birth experience, but we have found it can lead to disappointment for some when the plan does not come to fruition. Instead we recommend identifying birth preferences that state what is important to you in your birth experience, ways you can be supported, things that comfort you, and things that make you uncomfortable. It goes beyond medical procedures and interventions and focuses on how you want to feel during this transformative process. Ask yourself, how do you want to feel supported, empowered, listened to, and peaceful? By clearly identifying and articulating your desired emotions, you can develop a plan that aligns with your values and priorities.

Section Two: Choosing Your Birth Team

One of the crucial aspects of your birth plan is determining who you want to have by your side during the birthing process. Consider carefully who you want present at the hospital and immediately at home. These individuals will play an essential role in providing the support and comfort you need during this significant event in your life. By first identifying your birth preferences, you can think about who would best be able to support you and advocate for those preferences in the birth and postpartum period.

Let's take a moment to reflect

1 Take a moment to imagine your birth. How do you want to feel? Sometimes it can be easier to think of how you definitely don't want to feel as you explore this goal.

2 Who do you imagine being at the birth? Are there people you would like during labor vs during postpartum?

3 How would you like those around you to speak to you during labor?

4 How do you like to be comforted when you are in pain/scared?

Section Three: The Role of Hospital Key Players

When it comes to caring for you and your baby, several key players will be involved. Understanding their roles and establishing open lines of communication can contribute to a positive birthing experience. These key players may include:

- **Nurse**: The nurse will be your primary point of contact throughout your hospital stay. They will provide medical assistance, monitor your progress, and offer support.
- **Charge Nurse**: The charge nurse oversees the nursing staff and ensures the smooth operation of the labor and delivery unit.
- **Lactation Consultant**: Breastfeeding support is vital in the early days after birth. A lactation consultant can provide guidance and assistance to help you establish a successful breastfeeding relationship with your baby.
- **OB (Obstetrician)**: Your OB will be responsible for your prenatal care and will likely be present during the delivery. They will oversee any medical interventions, if necessary.
- **Midwife/Midlevel Provider**: If you have opted for midwifery care, a midwife or midlevel provider will guide you through the labor and delivery process. They specialize in providing personalized, holistic care during childbirth.

Creating your birth preferences that encompass both the health of your baby and your own well-being is an empowering step towards a positive birthing experience. By acknowledging the myth that "all that matters is a healthy baby," you can advocate for yourself and ensure that your needs are met throughout the journey to motherhood. Remember, your birth plan is a fluid document that allows for adjustments and flexibility. Trust in your instincts, communicate your desires clearly, and embrace the transformative experience of becoming a mother.

We encourage you to utilize the Birth Preferences template (p.112) accompanying this book as a way to verbalize these preferences you have identified for yourself.

"MOTHERHOOD IS SO MUCH MORE THAN THE DAY YOUR BABY IS YOUR BORN. YOUR BIRTH EXPERIENCE DOES NOT DEFINE YOU; GIVING BIRTH IS NOT THE ENDGAME."
-ASHLEE GADD

CHAPTER TEN

NAVIGATING THE WAVES:

Recognizing PMAD Symptoms &
Seeking the Right Support

Motherhood, just like the ocean, is full of ebbs and flows. This chapter is designed to guide you in navigating these waves, not by resisting them, but by learning to ride along with their rhythms. Much like mastering the art of surfing, it requires time, skill, and patience to adapt to these waves. But rest assured, as you garner knowledge and grow in understanding, you will gain the confidence to face each breaking wave with a steadfast plan, even when the weight of motherhood feels overwhelming.

Recognizing the signs of burnout, depression, and anxiety is your first step to effectively riding these waves. Our aim is to provide you with comprehensive, empathetic support and clear, concise information that will empower you to identify these signs and take positive action. Remember, you are not alone on this journey, and with the right tools, you can navigate the ups and downs of motherhood.

A Deeper Dive Into Perinatal Mood and Anxiety Disorders

Let's embark on the journey of understanding Perinatal Mood and Anxiety Disorders (PMADs). The term 'perinatal' encompasses the time from the onset of pregnancy through to one year after childbirth. In past discussions, the focus might have been primarily on Postpartum Depression, but our understanding has evolved. We now recognize that PMADs extend far beyond just postpartum depression.

The umbrella of PMADs covers a range of conditions, each with its own unique characteristics and effects on mothers. These include:

- **Depression and Anxiety** during the perinatal period
- **Perinatal Obsessive Compulsive Disorder**, a condition marked by intrusive, repetitive thoughts and compulsive behaviors

- **Perinatal Panic Disorder,** characterized by sudden, intense feelings of fear and physical symptoms like a racing heart or shortness of breath

- **Postpartum Post Traumatic Stress Disorder,** which can occur after a traumatic childbirth experience

- **Postpartum Psychosis,** a severe mental illness that includes symptoms like hallucinations and delusions, effecting 1-2 In 1,000 women

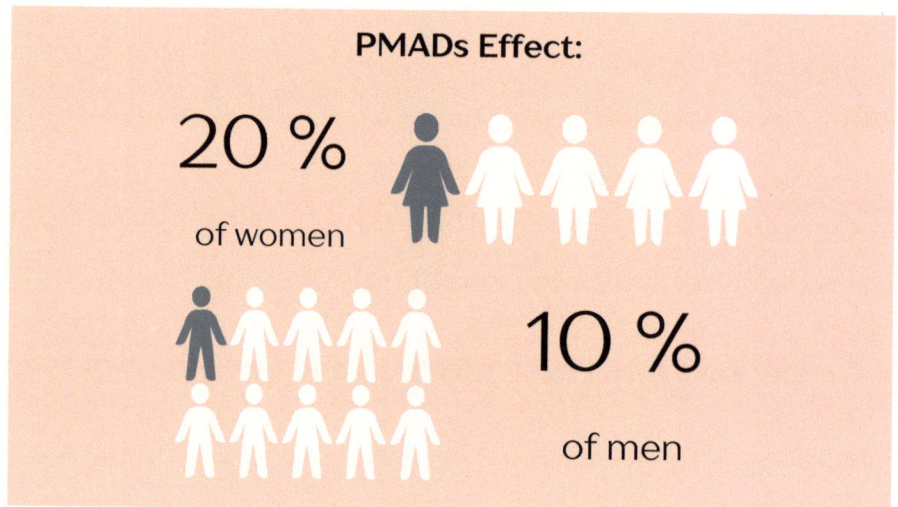

If left untreated, PMADs can potentially have the following impacts on families:

- Straining of relationships
- Worsening of existing medical conditions
- Risk of separation or divorce
- Potential loss of financial stability
- Possible unemployment or disability
- Risks to child welfare, including potential neglect or abuse
- Potential developmental delays in children
- Increased likelihood of alcohol or drug use
- Extreme cases may lead to infanticide, homicide, or suicide

Remember, it's never too early or too late to reach out for help. If at any point during your pregnancy, postpartum period, or even beyond, you feel a need for additional support, don't hesitate to seek assistance.

If symptoms start to interfere with your daily life or hinder your ability to care for yourself and prioritize rest, it becomes crucial to seek professional help. There are numerous resources available to assist you in these challenging times.

Let's explore a few of them:

- **Therapists:** These are Licensed Masters or PhD level clinicians who specialize in providing the necessary mental health support.
- **Psychiatrists:** Medical doctors (MDs) who specialize in offering medication-related support. While not all PMADs require medication, it can be a beneficial tool when used alongside therapy.
- **Support Groups:** Local community agencies often host support groups for postpartum mothers. Additionally, Postpartum Support International (PSI) offers a variety of free weekly support groups for pregnant and postpartum families.
- **Hotlines:** For immediate help, consider reaching out to:
  - PSI Helpline: 1-800-944-4773 (Available via call or text from 8am-11pm EST)
  - Suicide and Crisis Lifeline: 988 (Available 24/7)

Let's breakdown what some of the more recognizable PMADs may look like when you are experiencing them, and what others can see from the outside.

Baby Blues Effect 80% of new mothers
Occurs from birth through 2 weeks after birth

Baby Blues Can Look Like:
- Quick mood swings from happy to sad
- Not eating or taking care of yourself
- Crying frequently

Baby Blues Can Feel Like:
- Irritable
- Overwhelmed
- Anxious

Anxiety Can Look Like:
- Difficulty trusting others to care for baby
- Trouble falling asleep even when tired
- Increased forgetfulness
- Urges to check if baby is breathing

Anxiety Can Feel Like:
- Feeling out of control
- Feeling on edge
- Sore and tight muscles
- Feeling the need to do things "perfectly"
- Intrusive thoughts about things that could happen to baby

Depression Can Look Like:
- Little interest in seeing your friends or family
- Neglecting personal hygiene, not showering or brushing your teeth
- You're running on auto pilot, not truly shifting through highs and lows, more stuck in the lows
- Not eating or overeating

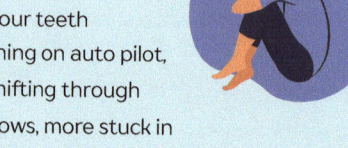

Depression Can Feel Like:
- Not feeling connected to your baby
- Having little energy or motivation
- Feeling like a horrible mother
- Feeling of heaviness and hopelessness

Psychosis Can Look Like:
- Auditory/visual hallucinations
- Delusions
- Rapid and irrational speech
- Little to no sleep, endless energy

Psychosis Can Feel Like:
- Paranoia and suspiciousness
- Thoughts of harm to you or those around you
- Confusion
- Difficulty Sleeping
- Feeling out of body
- Confusion
- Agitation

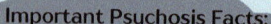

Important Psychosis Facts:
Typical onset Is 3-14 days postpartum
This Is a very treatable condition, seek medical attention ASAP

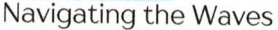

How you and your loved ones can talk about your mental health:

In the moment when we are struggling, it can be hard to know what's going on and get the courage to ask for help. Utilizing the information in this chapter and the postpartum mental health plans included in this book, we encourage you to talk to the support people in your life about signs you need support, signs you need to talk to a professional, and how you can communicate about these things in a way that feels loving and supportive. We recommend having a previously agreed upon prompt to make starting these conversations easier. This can look like:

Code Words that means we need to get in touch with the providers on my mental health plan. These can be something silly like *watermelon*. Code words are off the wall and often help our brain snap out of the thought pattern we might be entwined in. Using a code word can be helpful in many situations, in this situation in particular, to allow your partner to say "Hey, I see you are struggling and I want to get you help" without having to say all of those words. This allows your brain to receive the information, and likely respond in a less defensive way.

Phrases:
- I am really struggling and I think I need help from a doctor or therapist.
- I feel like I am not getting better after trying (**previously identified coping skills**), I think it is time to talk to my therapist.

Communication goes both ways. Think about now how you like to be approached when you need help, or when your partner notices you are struggling emotionally. We can understand the vulnerability and courage it takes to allow your partner or support person to help you in a time that feels so uncertain. Thinking ahead of a phrase or way your partner can communicate their worry and need for you to seek additional support will help if that time comes and help you approach the situation with a clear head.

At the end of this chapter we have Included a Postpartum Mental Health Plan for both you and your partner. Completing this plan is similar to an Insurance policy, It's better to have It and not need It, then need It and not have It.

In the Postpartum Mental Health Plan, you have the opportunity to identify two key supporters. Your partner may be an immediate choice, but consider a second supporter who is close, yet somewhat removed from the everyday hustle with your newborn. This person can provide a fresh perspective and notice if you're struggling.

As we continue to explore the plan, you'll be able to enlist your Professional Support team – this could include your OB/GYN, therapist, doula, or community leader.

Then, we delve into self care strategies. Imagine these as 'Red Day' strategies from our Self Care Stop Light. They are simple, achievable, and designed to help you reconnect with yourself.

Following this, if your self care strategies aren't yielding the desired results, consider this next step as a pact between you and your support persons. You consent to them scheduling an appointment with your chosen professional support and discuss how they can assist you until that appointment.

If securing an appointment is proving difficult, or if you're experiencing thoughts of self-harm or harm to others, please dial 988 at any hour to connect with the Suicide and Crisis hotline. If you're not in crisis but require support, you can reach out to the Postpartum Support International Help Line at 1-800-944-4773 (available via call or text from 8 am–11 pm EST).

Navigating this plan might seem daunting, especially when anticipating potential challenges like 'what if I experience xyz'. Please remember, by engaging with this book and formulating this plan, you've already overcome the toughest hurdles. Your courage to take these initial steps is commendable.

Let's conclude this chapter with a crucial topic: Parental Burnout - how to identify it and overcome it.

Parental burnout is a term first coined by Belgian psychologists Isabelle Roskam and Moïra Mikolajczak in the early 1980s. It's characterized by three main features:

- Overwhelming exhaustion linked to your parenting role.
- Emotional distancing from your children.
- A sense of ineffectiveness or uncertainty about your parenting abilities.

Recent studies reveal that up to 68% of mothers and 42% of fathers meet the criteria for parental burnout. Symptoms, similar to untreated PMADs mentioned earlier, include:

- Constant fatigue and drained energy.
- Emotional detachment.
- Loss of interest in previously enjoyed activities.
- Persistent irritability and frustration.
- Feelings of entrapment or a desire to escape.
- Perceived inadequacy as a parent.

The primary cause of burnout? An imbalance between parenting-related stressors and stress relievers.

Factors that can increase risk include:

- Striving for perfection in parenting.
- Having a child with special needs.
- Both parents working outside the home.
- Lack of support from extended family or childcare.
- Difficulty asking for help.

On the flip side, protective factors include:

- Practicing self-compassion.
- Taking breaks from parenting duties.
- Maintaining a strong relationship through quality alone time.
- Receiving external support from family, childcare, etc.
- The ability to recognize when you're feeling low and reaching out for help.

How can you prevent or mitigate parental burnout once it starts to take hold?

Firstly, don't hesitate to ask for help. Identify a trusted support network, perhaps one or two people who can step in when you're feeling overwhelmed. They can help care for your child(ren), providing you with much-needed respite.

Secondly, cultivate a practice of self-compassion. Be gentle with yourself and remember that no parent is perfect. Embrace the imperfections as part of your unique parenting journey. As a Fulfilled Mama, you are already demonstrating strength and resilience.

Remember, the beauty of motherhood lies not in perfection, but in the authentic love and care you provide. You are exactly the right mother for your family, shaped by your experiences and rooted in your individual strengths.

In closing, navigating the waves of motherhood can be a challenging, yet rewarding journey. It's important to remember that it's normal to experience ups and downs. However, when you find yourself stuck in a cycle of overwhelming exhaustion, emotional distancing, or feelings of inadequacy, reach out for support. Remember, you're not alone.

Hey There Mama,

We're thrilled to see you finish "The Confident Postpartum"! Thank you for allowing us to accompany you on this precious journey into motherhood.

As you step forward, remember to celebrate the unique, incredible woman you are. Motherhood is more than just ticking off a list of "mom" tasks. It's about fully embracing your individuality and showing up as YOU.

You are now part of our Fulfilled Mama community. To us, you are a superhero. You are strong, resilient, and unafraid to carve out your own path. You understand that there's no universal manual for being a mom – and that's perfectly fine. You exude confidence, set your own standards, and shine with a sense of self-assured contentment.

Our workbook was designed to support you in becoming this "Fulfilled Mama". We hope it has equipped you with valuable tools, insights, and a generous dose of self-belief to navigate motherhood with assurance. It's perfectly normal to have questions, doubts, and fears. But remember, you now possess a strong foundation and a supportive community to lean on.

Please stay connected! We'd love to hear about your progress and experiences. Follow us on Instagram @fulfilling.motherhood – we're always here to chat, provide support, and celebrate each step you take on this remarkable journey.

Once again, thank you. Here's to you, mama, and to the exciting, fulfilling journey that lies ahead!

Sending you all the love and positive vibes,

Krysta & Sarah

P.S.– Don't forget to check out the worksheets after this! They are great tools to take out of the book and have on hand. If you want to download and print them, head over to fulfillingmotherhood.com/worksheets

WORKSHEETS &
TAKEAWAYS

Visit fulfillingmotherhood.com/worksheets

for a downloadable version

MOM'S POSTPARTUM MENTAL HEALTH PLAN

MY CORE SUPPORT

CORE SUPPORT #1:	CORE SUPPORT #2:

MY PROFESSIONAL SUPPORT

OB/GYN OR MIDWIFE:	THERAPIST:	PRIMARY CARE:
Name:	Name:	Name:
Phone:	Phone:	Phone:

OTHER SUPPORT (DOULA, RELIGIOUS LEADER, COMMUNITY LEADER)
NAME: PHONE:

SELF CARE STRATEGIES

IF MY SELF CARE STRATEGIES AREN'T EFFECTIVE

PHYSICAL ACTIVITY I ENJOY DOING:	I WOULD LIKE MY CORE SUPPORT PERSON:
A MEAL THAT MAKES MY BODY FEEL NOURISHED:	TO HELP ME MAKE AN APPOINTMENT WITH MY PROFESSIONAL SUPPORT:
HOW CAN I REST IN THE NEXT 24 HOURS:	UNTIL MY APPOINTMENT, MY CORE SUPPORT CAN HELP ME BY:

PSI HELPLINE: 1-800-944-4773 (CALL OR TEXT FROM 8AM–11PM EST)
SUICIDE AND CRISIS LIFELINE: 988

PARTNER'S POSTPARTUM SUPPORT PLAN

MY CORE SUPPORT

CORE SUPPORT #1:

CORE SUPPORT #2:

MY PROFESSIONAL SUPPORT

PRIMARY CARE:

Name:

Phone:

THERAPIST:

Name:

Phone:

SELF CARE STRATEGIES

PHYSICAL ACTIVITY I ENJOY DOING:

A MEAL THAT MAKES MY BODY FEEL NOURISHED:

HOW CAN I REST IN THE NEXT 24 HOURS:

IF MY SELF CARE STRATEGIES AREN'T EFFECTIVE

I WOULD LIKE MY CORE SUPPORT PERSON:

TO HELP ME MAKE AN APPOINTMENT WITH MY PROFESSION SUPPORT:

UNTIL MY APPOINTMENT, MY CORE SUPPORT CAN HELP ME BY:

PSI HELPLINE: 1-800-944-4773 (CALL OR TEXT FROM 8AM–11PM EST)
SUICIDE AND CRISIS LIFELINE: 988

We understand that discussing your mental health with a healthcare professional can feel intimidating. To assist you in this process, we've created a dedicated space for you to jot down any thoughts, feelings, or concerns you might wish to share. You can bring this with you during your appointment or simply take a snapshot on your phone for easy reference. This can help facilitate a more open and beneficial conversation at your next visit.

I have been experiencing the following symptoms:

Since approximately:

I sometimes feel better when:

I sometimes feel worse when:

Notes:

THE _____

FAMILY VALUES

ESTABLISHED ON:

1

2

3

4

5

OVERNIGHT SLEEP PLANNING

Time	
5 pm	
6 pm	
7 pm	
8 pm	
9 pm	
10 pm	
11 pm	
12 am	
1 am	
2 am	
3 am	
4 am	
5 am	
6 am	
7 am	
8 am	
9 am	
10 am	

Birth Preferences

Quick Info

Name

Support Persons

I am...

Excited about:

Scared about:

Curious about:

What brings me comfort:

What makes me uncomfortable:

A note to my providers:

I have noted my birth preferences on the back of this page. I understand that birth at times can be unpredictable.

If we need to deviate from my preferences, please let me know any alternatives, risks/benefits, and reasoning. Giving me time to digest info and ask questions will help me stay confident during delivery.

Your empathy makes all the difference. Thanks for being part of this journey!

Do Not Disturb:

Code Word/Phrase:

During Labor I would like to feel:

- [ ] Empowered
- [ ] Confident
- [ ] Assured
- [ ] Informed
- [ ] Included
- [ ] Supported
- [ ] Surrounded by love
- [ ] Peaceful
- [ ] Understood

During Labor:

- [ ] Dimmed Lights
- [ ] Music (I have a playlist)
- [ ] I would like to be out of bed as much as possible.
- [ ] I will have a photographer present.

Labor Tools:

- [ ] Birthing Ball
- [ ] CUB Support
- [ ] Peanut Balls
- [ ] Squat Bars
- [ ] Shower

Pain Control:

- [ ] Epidural
- [ ] Walking Epidural
- [ ] No medical pain Intervention
- [ ] I am unsure
- [ ] I will use breathing exercises, massage, showers, etc.

Delivery Method:

- [ ] Vaginal
- [ ] C-Section
- [ ] VBAC

During Delivery:

- [ ] I would like to delay cord clamping.
- [ ] I would like a mirror.
- [ ] I would like to touch my baby's head as It crowns.
- [ ] I would like my partner to cut the umbilical cord.

Newborn Care:

Feeding Preference:
- [ ] Breast
- [ ] Formula
- [ ] Mixed
- [ ] I would like to give the first bath.

Circumcision:
- [ ] Yes
- [ ] No
- [ ] Please discharge us home as soon as possible.

What I need Postpartum:

- [ ] To take a shower as soon as I can.
- [ ] Long periods to sleep uninterrupted.
- [ ] To change in to my clothes.
- [ ] Time to slow down and be with baby.
- [ ] Time to eat.
- [ ] _____

Other Important things to know:

During Labor I would like to feel:

- ☐ _____
- ☐ _____
- ☐ _____

- ☐ _____
- ☐ _____
- ☐ _____

During Labor:

- ☐ _____
- ☐ _____
- ☐ _____
- ☐ _____
- ☐ _____

Labor Tools:

- ☐ _____
- ☐ _____
- ☐ _____

Pain Control:

- ☐ _____
- ☐ _____
- ☐ _____
- ☐ _____
- ☐ _____

Delivery Method:

- ☐ _____
- ☐ _____
- ☐ _____

Newborn Care:

Feeding Preference:
- ☐ _____

Circumcision:
- ☐ _____
- ☐ _____
- ☐ _____

During Delivery:

- ☐ _____
- ☐ _____
- ☐ _____
- ☐ _____

What I need Postpartum:

- ☐ _____
- ☐ _____
- ☐ _____

- ☐ _____
- ☐ _____
- ☐ _____

Other Important things to know:

SELF CARE STOP LIGHT

Now that you have an idea of the things that you enjoy, let's take a minute to break out what an Ideal, Moderate, and Quick and Easy Self Care day will look like for you. Having this will help take the mental load out of planning out your self care. Simply Identify what color day it is and follow the plan you have already set.

Green Light – Ideal Self Care

Yellow Light – Moderate Self Care

Red Light – Quick and Easy Self Care

A quick guide to having Fulfilling T.A.L.K.S.

T   Types and Styles of Communication

A   Awareness of Self and Others

L   Listening actively

K   Kindness in Communication

S   Silence & Non-Verbal Signals

Positive Affirmations for Pregnancy, Birth, and Postpartum

You are a strong and courageous woman.

My partner and I are in this together. We will shift and adjust as a team.

You are doing everything you can for yourself and your baby.

You're going to be a wonderful parent.

My baby and I are a team.

I trust my body to know what to do.

Each surge of my body brings my baby closer to me.

I am prepared to meet whatever turns my birthing takes.

Birth is powerful. I will let it empower me.

I am present. I am doing this. We are doing this.

Motherhood has shown me my strengths.

This is a resting period for me and my baby. And that is okay.

I do not have to enjoy every moment of this period.

I am new to this. It is okay that I make mistakes.

I am doing a great job.

While you're here visiting with our new family, we would appreciate help with ANYTHING on this list. It would be such a lifesaver for us! Thank you!

SMALL TASK	MEDIUM TASK	LARGER TASK

Want to explore some of our favorite thought leaders mentioned throughout the book? Check them out here:

Fair Play, Eve Rodsky
More info: https://www.fairplaylife.com/

Postpartum Support International, 1.800.944.4773
More info: https://www.postpartum.net/

The Gottman Institute, John and Julie Gottman
More info: https://www.gottman.com/

The Motherhood Experiences of Non-Birth Mothers in Same-Sex Parent Families. McInerney, A., Creaner, M., & Nixon, E. (2021).
More info: Psychology of Women Quarterly, 45(3), 279–293. https://doi.org/10.1177/03616843211003072

Transition to Fatherhood, Sonia Molloy, Brian Cole, Alyssa Dye, and Danny Singley, The Pennsylvania State University
More info: https://pure.psu.edu/en/publications/transition-to-fatherhood

www.ingramcontent.com/pod-product-compliance
Lightning Source LLC
Chambersburg PA
CBHW041454120626
46547CB00003B/438